TAPESTRY OF MY SOUL

REBIRTHING THE SACRED SEXUAL FEMININE MYSTERIES

BY
ROBIN "OSUNNIKE" SCOTT-MANNA
aka Queen Mother Osunnike Anke

Tapestry of My Soul: Rebirthing the Sacred Sexual Feminine Mysteries
Copyright © 2022 Robin "Osunnike" Scott-Manna

Paperback ISBN: 979-8-9856592-6-9
Kindle ISBN: 979-8-9856592-7-6

All rights reserved. No portion of this book may be reproduced or utilized in any form, or by any electronic, mechanical, or other means, without the prior written permission from the author. This book is for entertainment purposes only. This publication is sold with the understanding that neither the author nor publisher is engaged in rendering legal, accounting, financial, or other professional service. If legal advice or other expert assistance is required, the services of a competent professional person should be sought. Although the Publisher and Author have made every effort to ensure the information in this book was correct at press time, neither assumes and hereby disclaims any liability for any loss, damage, or disruption caused by this book. The author, publisher, and/or distributors are not responsible for any adverse effects resulting from the use of the suggestions outlined in this book.

Published by RITZ BOOKS
Cover art drawing by Dara Imani Bayer
Cover design, author headshots, and book layout by Steph Ritz

RitzBooks.com guides authors to create books, courses, stage talks, websites, marketing, and educational materials for professional development, self-improvement, and online learning. We support entrepreneurs, business professionals, and industry leaders to voice their passions – with ghostwriting, editing, graphic design, copywriting, photography, publishing, and more. Do you have a book idea, or have you already written a book manuscript you'd like us to consider publishing?

Please visit **StephRitz.com** to learn more.
Or email **Steph@StephRitz.com** to get started today.

TABLE OF CONTENTS

Beginning with the End in Mind 4

About the Author 6

Part ONE Know Thyself 8

Chapter One ~ Do You Know Who You Are? ~ 12

Chapter Two ~ Collecting My Soul's Threads ~ 32

Chapter Three ~ My Introduction to Sacred Sexuality ~ 39

Part TWO Cleansing and Purifying 50

Chapter Four ~ Osun, African Tantric Goddess ~ 52

Chapter Five ~ Initiation? Really?! Yes Really! ~ 63

Chapter Six ~ Recovering from the Fall from Grace ~ 68

Part THREE Living in Alignment with Absolute Truth 76

Chapter Seven ~ Honoring Me First, then My Beloved Came Along ~ 80

Chapter Eight ~ Not Kentucky Fried Chicken ~ 87

Chapter Nine ~ Yes, I Know Who I Am ~ 114

Finale ~ The Divine Cosmic Womb Blueprint ~ 138

We End at Your Beginning 147

Interactive Multimedia Bonuses 153

Work with Queen Mother Osunnike 156

Beginning with the End in Mind

The Evolving Self

During my early years as an actor, poet, short story writer and playwright, I would spend countless hours rehearsing lines, identifying, and perfecting my characters' traits, developing intricate plots and storylines, making sure that they were believable, realistic and of star quality. However, more importantly, I learned that a great story always begins with the "end in mind". Even if the ending changed once you got there, you at least needed to have some clue up front about how you wanted your story and your main character to end up.

Looking back at my childhood, all my countless character preparations and childish "wanna be" academy award winning performances were a mere reflection of how we as humans are really acting out our lives on the cosmic stage, screen, and best-selling book called, "Life". You see this spiritual knowledge and awareness only began to unfold for me when I had consciously made a serious commitment to assume responsibility for my own life. It was time to stop being a victim, listen intently, and begin to intimately study and consciously know my evolving "higher" self from the inside out.

Let me begin by sharing why we are called to "Begin with the End in Mind".

Our universe is undergoing an Evolutionary and Planetary shift and we're in a time of major transition, and the momentum is building across the world to consciously "begin rebirthing a new world". During this Earthy Ascension, "it's time" my sister as "CEEW" (Consciously Evolving

Empowered Women) to remember, reignite, and reclaim your hidden Sacred Feminine Powerful Treasures, which are your inherent birthright, deeply embedded within your womb.

My current lifetime journey has guided me to remember, reawaken and reignite the seeds of The Sacred Sexual Feminine Mysteries sheathed within my womb and many wombs around the world.

As we heal our wombs, we will naturally contribute to the healing of the womb of our "Earth Mother", and her human family; for one mother's womb is another mother's womb.

Now, let me share some of the design nuggets of *Tapestry of My Soul – Rebirthing the Sacred Sexual Feminine Mysteries* with you:

Tapestry of My Soul is being shared with you as a perfectly imperfect mosaic that retraces the fragmented blueprint of my soul. Yes, it mirrors my raw, vulnerable tender sacred feminine power, brilliance, and resilience. Intertwined into *Tapestry of My Soul* is other-worldly imagery, and flashbacks of my past lifetimes, flavored with present lifetime insights of my African American, Cherokee, Indigenous and Ancestral Intergenerational past and present soul journeys. By retracing the footprints of my soul's journey through my personal mythology, this book magically weaves my soul's fragmented returns into a mosaic reflecting personal and spiritual healing, liberation, and human transcendence back into my original greatness, spiritual perfection, and ultimately wholeness/the perfect sacred union from the inside out.

Tapestry of My Soul uses my poetry, rhythmic movement, and the whispered echoes of my spiritual and ancestral guides as a mirror to inspire you to remember your Sacred Sexual Feminine origins, incarnation and to re-weave the *Tapestry of Your Soul*.

Let's do this!

About the Author

Queen Mother Osunnike Anke is a natural healer, spiritual intuitive/seeress, priestess of the ancient West African goddess Osun, co-founder and president of the **Institute of Whole Life Healing**, a non-profit designed to assist individuals and groups in remembering their Original Greatness, Life's Purpose, and Divinity.

Queen Mother Osunnike's passionate life's purpose for over 30 years is creatively assisting women in healing and transmuting mind, body, ancestral, social, sexual, and cultural trauma so they can liberate the dormant **Sacred Transformative Power** within their wombs. She KNOWS that as healed, whole, liberated, and UNITED women – we have the Innate POWER to change our world. In alignment with her life's purpose and Inner Knowing, she was called to birth **One Million Wombs United (OMWU).** OMWU is a universal mission uniquely designed to reignite the **Sacred Feminine** luminosity within the wombs of a "critical mass" of Consciously Evolving Empowered Women called to give birth to a New World. Additionally, she is a Reiki Master, sound vibration healer, psycho-spiritual therapist, published author, and performance artist.

She is also the Chief Priestess of the **Sacred Feminine Mysteries Initiation – Passage into The Great Mother Priesthood,** a sacred initiatory process, during which she is the spiritual midwife to "chosen" women in honoring their "Inner Spiritual Covenant" with **The Great Mother** in service to humanity.

These initiations are uniquely designed and facilitated to guide you into balance and harmony with your feminine nature and offer you an opportunity to reclaim your sacred feminine legacy, personal power, and divine inheritance. This can help you consciously contribute healthier womb and heart centered energy to your family, community, humanity, and our Earth Mother.

Within these Sacred Feminine Mysteries initiations and many of the retreats, Queen Mother Osunnike often utilizes the "Beginning with the End in Mind – The Evolving Self" as an interactive writing and performance model, which will ask the question: What if this role you are playing is just that – a role?

Queen Mother Osunnike is gifted with the unique ability to genuinely connect with people from all walks of life. As she traverses the universe from Peru to Africa, she effortlessly encircles people in her magically woven tapestry of love, grace, and spiritual truth, while healing hearts and wombs. Affectionately known as the "healers' healer", her work is truly a luminous reflection of her diverse life's journey, purpose, and natural gifts.

One Million Wombs United
http://www.onemillionwombsunited.org/

Institute of Whole Life Healing
www.manypaths1truth.org

Part ONE
Know Thyself

**I Can't Wait to Know
What it Really Means
to be the Daughter of...**

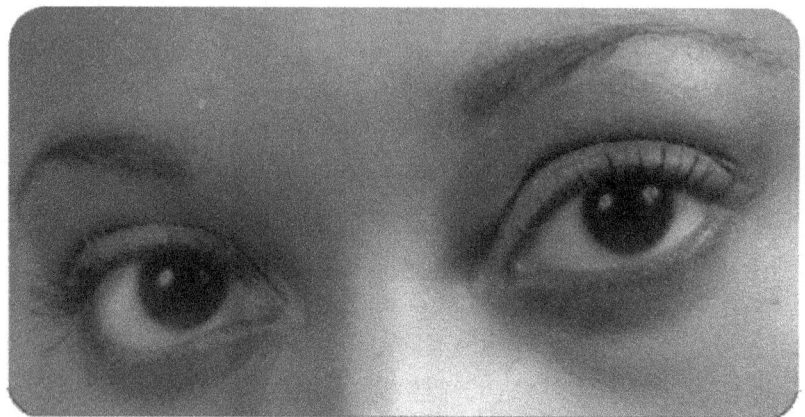

Am I My Mother's Daughter?

Oh, my dear mother...

What does it mean to be your daughter?

What does that carry?

I know that I cannot carry the anger, guilt or shame that has been the most memorable bond between us for so long.

Oh, my dear mother...

I want to dive into the treasures of what appears to be a very rich legacy.

There is so much I need to know, and you have always been bigger than life to me.

So now that your physical life has ended, what do I do with my gigantic memory of you.

Oh, my dear mother...

I guess I thought you would live forever and now that you, and daddy are both physically gone I'm finding it very hard to believe that I am motherless and fatherless.

Oh, my dear mother...

How do I continue my connection with you and to you?

I know that you both will be ever present with me.

Yet, it is so hard for me to believe that physically you're gone from my life because there's so much, I still don't know about you... the life which gave me life.

I really need to know.

Who were you... on the inside?

Where did you get your confidence from and your drive for life and for God?

Oh, my dear mother...

I am your daughter, and I don't really know what that means.

Who are you and why did I choose your womb?

I wanted so much to know all of who you are... because I can't really know who I am, without knowing all of who you are.

Right now, all I have are the fragmented pieces of our life together... disjointed pieces of our lives.

Oh, my dear mother...

Who are you?

I witnessed your never wavering strength and your magnanimous spirit.

But who are you?

Oh, my dear mother...

I knew all too well your disappointment with me, and your sadness that I didn't devote my life to Your God in the way that you did.

But there has to be more... I know there has to be more.

I knew your incredible faith in God.

But never knew your faith in me and who I am.

So, my dear mother…

I have to put these scattered pieces of our lives together without your physical help…

Perhaps now we can talk and share in spiritual ways that we just couldn't do before.

Mom…

Help me mend this tattered and torn tapestry of my soul and I promise that our spiritual legacy will be a sacred tapestry that will live on forever.

And we are… because I remembered the truth of who I really am. Well not right away.

Chapter One
~ Do You Know Who You Are? ~

I, the second daughter, was divinely conceived from the sacred union between Pentecostal Missionary, Evangelist, Shepherdess Naomi Jace Drayton; a spiritually anointed woman, divinely yoked first and foremost to God "our father" who art in heaven. Secondly, she was yoked with Reverend, Elder, Pastor William Robert Scott; a majestically handsome and world traveled man gifted with quite a bit of intellectual prowess. Perhaps their titles and calling formed some of my earlier lifelong challenges stemmed from - Dogmatic Religion - hint hint! Anyway, I was birthed from my mother's sacred womb into my present lifetime during the zodiacal sign of Gemini, in the gentle heat of the late night, before the summer solstice. I know now that my mother intuitively knew that her physical womb was naturally and energetically infused with the nucleus (blueprint) to procreate goddesses and gods – that is with the "right" earthly man. Naomi was the only child born from my Nana, Sara's womb, and there were stories regarding Nana and the "right" earthly man that I wouldn't know until much later.

So, in my earlier years I would ask myself how could such a divine experience become so emotionally jacked-up for me? I mean all birth is sacred – right? Wasn't mine? I mean wasn't I there? What the hell happened, because my early life wasn't a reflection of the divine sacred union between Naomi and William. Over the years I was haunted with the need to know where these incessant feelings of needing to feel special, deprivation, abandonment, emotional insecurity, and self-doubt were rising out of?

However, along my journey, I began to unfold the knowing

that as our mothers' daughters, we carry the encoded past and present lifetime genetic memories of their ancestral mothers' lineage, legacy, baggage, and resilience within our sacred wombs stretching seven generations back and destined to travel at least seven generations forward.

It's so amazing that our physical wombs are these complex incubators that are designed to nurture, nourish, and evolve our mind, body temples and spirit. Therefore, it's essential for us as women to heal our womb's ancestral, present day, and past-life trauma. The umbilical cord and placenta are the energetic lifeline to ensure that the proper ingredients are delivered for optimum mind, body, spiritual development, and self-mastery. So, to tap back into the divine knowledge, wisdom, and cosmic intelligence of and within the womb, we must consciously reactivate our "umbilical communication" which is our spiritual and kinesthetic lifeline to our embryonic divinity. When we tap into our divinity through this lifeline, we are tapping into our genetic antennae that brings the past, present, and future remnants into the now as a tapestry reflecting our soul's journey.

Looking back over my tapestry, I grew into a playfully inquisitive seeker of truth with deep brown eyes, almost too big for my face, mirrors reflecting the wonderment of my soul's journey – at least thus far. I was born pre-wired with an innocently creative and anciently inquisitive mind that needed to question and "know" the backstory behind and in front of just about every story. True to my nature, I often questioned the circumstances surrounding my birth – "I mean was I an accident, divinely planned or really wanted?" For real, this was a part of my childhood internal questioning.

Back in the mid-1940s, I would say that my parents Naomi and William who were 27 and 30 when they first met, already had lifestyles that weren't necessarily suited for each other; let alone marriage and beginning a family. My beautiful, sophisticated college-educated virgin mother, who preferred to live at home with her parents, had at the age of thirteen fully given herself to the only man worthy of her – the begotten son of God – yes, Jesus Christ himself.

She knew her womb was special and was clear that no other man could come close to winning her heart and especially her body, like Jesus had. Well, I take that back. The only other man, who was a possible husband candidate before my dad, blew that proposal out the window when his pre-marital blood test came back positive for syphilis. Any concerns she may have had about being an "old maid" after that were null and void as she said, "thank you Jesus!"

And her natural maternal instincts were honored and expressed as a teacher at the Harriet Tubman House Nursery School. Now, my handsome college-educated debonair father on the other hand, had travelled around the world in the Merchant Marines, Coast Guard and Navy as an officer and a chef, and was very well seasoned on all fronts. He had taken the marriage plunge once before and was now a dedicated single man living next door to my mother in Miss Becky's rooming house.

Even with their proximity and all my father's charm and military determination, after 3 years of trying, it did not win him a romantic date with my mother. I remember her telling my sister and me about how my father saw her walking down the street one rainy day. To her utter amazement, he removed his jacket and laid it over a puddle in front of her so she wouldn't get her shoes wet. "If you want to have a conversation with me, be ready for church this Sunday." He tried several other tactics. All were met with the same response. So, he finally surrendered and followed her to church to meet Jesus and the pastor, and a few months later, the rest was history in the making.

Yet, even after holy matrimony took place, the long-awaited honeymoon union was too painful to complete. But my dad endured and even after accepting Jesus, he would only be able to hold her hand, even though he had to leave and go back overseas a few days later. Finally, my sister Doreen was conceived 3 months later and somehow and some way I came along SEVEN years later. Who spaced their children's births out seven years back in those days? I wondered over the years what was this tapestry connecting my mother, her mother and me?

I can remember over the years hearing my mother often very proudly state, "Your daddy and I were so pleased when you came along." I was thinking my daddy was probably exhausted. He was 41 and back overseas working as a cook on the ship, having to support a family from afar, prove to his wife that God didn't make a mistake having her choose him, and now, another daughter seven years later is about to enter his world – ME. Now, what on Mother Earth could that have been about?

By the time I was born my mother had moved us into 14 Arnold Street, the new house she was able to buy, which I only have a few memories of, before the raging house fire burned them all away. It was the house where life began for me outside of the womb just one street over from my Nana. My nana, who I defined as my savior and hero, may have legitimately earned that title when my mother was forced to abruptly stop nursing me during the first year of my life. My sister and I were sure that Nana must have taken on the responsibility for feeding us and taking care of our mother. The beginning of my "nursing deprivation" turned into an ongoing story of mom's indestructible faith, dedication and devotion that became the signature testimony she shared with hundreds of people needing to strengthen their faith in the lord.

She would proudly recount how as a baby my strong gums bit into her breast, which resulted in an abscess forming. She refused repeatedly to seek medical care even when it became infected. Instead, she would lift her head high and emphatically state that she was determined to wait on the lord – even when the pastor advised – I think it's time to go to the hospital missionary Scott. "No.", she would cry out as she methodically tore out special scriptures from the bible and laid them on her breast with holy oil, as she prayed and prayed into the heavens, while waiting for her miracle, which by the way did happen. Her breast healed but, in the meantime, who the hell was feeding me, became my internalized rant. This is a question I asked my sister over the years and we both concluded it must have been my Nana. A year later, my mother was so proud of me because I won the Carnation Evaporated Milk Healthy Baby Contest. Go figure!

The next four to five years of my life centered around 6 Gannett Street where my parents, who were now fully invested in their lives together as minister and missionary of a small budding church, which by the way just happened to be housed in what had been our spacious and beautiful living and dining rooms. Now, this tiny church and what it represented became bigger than life in my eyes. Everything in my world was bigger than life and trying to relate to the people, places and things who were very much a part of my life became slightly intimidating – except for my Nana that is.

However, my mother became an excellent buffer between me and the realities of the world; whatever those realities were. You see I didn't even realize I had any needs outside of the basic ones because my mother met them all, whether I asked or not. Perhaps that early nurturing that was dramatically interrupted was now being overcompensated by feeding me everything SHE thought I needed, whether I needed it or not. This over nurturing fed a growing distorted sense of not being or having enough, which ultimately began to nourish an ongoing feeling of deprivation no matter what I was feeding on or off of. Inside my belly this "not enough" was turning into too much. I desperately needed a space where I was lovingly JUST ENOUGH.

That physical space was at Nana's house. There I began to treasure my solitude and being with my Nana, who loved me unconditionally – like GOD "should have" – and fantasized on far away lushly beautiful ancient places and blissful interludes of love with my faceless and nameless beloved.

Even as a young girl, I, an incurable romantic and idealist, would sit for hours envisioning the face of my heavenly lover who would whisk me into the arms of sweet reunion. Then, at every Sunday service, I was forced to come back into my parents' reality. I remember every Sunday as a little girl standing at the piano with brother Horton, who was struggling from last night's hangover, playing as I struggled to sing my mother's favorite chosen song for me. "Yes, Jesus loves me. Yes, Jesus loves me. Yes, Jesus loves me for the Bible tells me so. Little ones to him belong; they are weak, but he is strong. Jesus loves me this I know, as he loved so long ago. Taking children on his knee; saying let them come to me. Yes, Jesus loves me. Yes, Jesus loves me. Yes, Jesus loves me, so the Bible tells me so." The innocence of my tender love that I felt so deeply from my cosmic fairytale lover was then invaded by the rambling biblical threats of an angry, hypocritical, jealous god and his smooth-talking son who demanded my unconditional love and devotion, while contradicting every morsel of truth my family struggled to believe in and uphold through good moral character, church, and community service.

I later realized that the difference between what I experienced when I was at my Nana's house, which felt more real and manageable, and when I was at home with my parents was like an exaggerated night and day experience.

Nana's house was big and old
the staircase
I believed
went all the way up to the sky
boy how I love to climb
up those stairs
Nana's house was big and old
and safe
I could wander
in and out
of those rooms
up and down
the stairs
in and out
of the big closets
the closets
that was the most amount of fun
Nana had two big trunks
filled
with tons and tons and tons of old clothes
I could dress up
and play

and be
and play
and wander
and climb and climb and climb and…

So, through my "not enough" big brown eyes, viewing this bigger than life reality I slipped into an incredible vivid imaginary world of a staircase that took me to where I was "more than enough" in Nana's house.

Then, back home, as if I were in the movies, I knew when to cry, laugh, smile, pout and, most importantly, lie. I cultivated the skill set of lying, lying about my feelings, lying on my sister, lying about my needs, and creating elaborate stories with characters who told incredible lies to each other within their stories. I had developed an incredible imagination and liberated a latent and dormant gift for storytelling, which depending on who was telling the story, could also be viewed as lies. Together with my insatiable inborn need to be in the know, I also began to intuitively sense the lies that were being spoken as indisputable truths supposedly from God. And through my big brown eyes, those lies were even more incredulous than mine.

The biggest lies that I heard again and again (back then) from the dogmatic Pentecostal religious mouth pieces for God, and ultimately came to challenge, even as a young child, was the code of conduct that determined what it meant to be a saint. This code was also what got you into the pearly gates of heaven, and as a sinner, the horrible punishment that damned your soul to hell. Worship a God, "they" said, who loved the world so much that he allowed Jesus, his only begotten son, to die in vain for the sins of a people that my young ancient soul just intuitively knew my ancestral clan had never committed against humanity. I mean, what happened to the "forgiveness and unconditional love"? Oh, what a struggle at such a young and tender age to know what I really wasn't supposed to know, yet. Yes, I hated growing up Pentecostal. I longed to return to a time beyond before, a time when I was free, old, young, brand new, and it was ok to be wise, wise, innocently wise.

For the first eleven years of my life my Nana was as good as you can get in honoring my innocent wisdom. In many ways, she and my Papa mirrored many of the good deeds that my parents exemplified. Although Nana and Papa were not active "Baptist" churchgoers, they were all about helping and supporting others within their community. I later realized that my grandparents much like my parents provided comfortable rooms and meals for folks who didn't have a place for whatever reason to live in at the time.

In their big old three-story brownstone house, they provided living space for Miss Bessie, Uncle Johnny, Uncle Bob, Mr. Burnett, and maybe one or two others whose names I don't remember now. I'm not even sure whether Uncle Johnny was a real uncle because back in those days, we were just told to refer to some elders as auntie and uncle.

When I look back now, I see Uncle Johnny smoking his cigar and Uncle Bob sitting in the living room watching their favorite western series The Lone Ranger and The Rifle Man and arguing about which one was best. Slightly annoyed, I would keep glancing at the clock on the wall because I did not want to miss my favorite western series – Zorro. As Nana called to Uncle Johnny and Uncle Bob, "Come on now, come on now, food is ready."

I was torn between the mouthwatering smell of Nana's Carolina rice and black-eyed peas, sweet cornbread, and watching Uncle Johnny blowing smoke circles from his cigar and Uncle Bob's stuttering angry rants about the Rifle Man being the best man. However, in the midst of this bigger than life scene in Nana's living room, I sure didn't want to miss my favorite scenes with my handsome, sophisticated, debonaire, fierce fantasy boyfriend, Zorro who made sure he took good care of those pretty ladies before he rode off into the sunset.

Then I would hear Nana calling me, "Come on girl; turn that tv off. Come on, come on before your food gets cold.

"Okay!" So, if I had to choose between Nana and Zorro, dang, it was going to be Nana.

Yeah, I loved being at Nana's house but where the houses differed, they really differed. Another thing I loved about being at Nana's house was watching my Nana and her two best friends Miss Mary and Miss Pearl play cards, drink just a little bit of whiskey and dance to the blues at least once a month. Of course, my Nana didn't know that after she put me to bed, kissed me good night and placed the room divider between me and all the action that sleep was the last thing I wanted to do. Oh no! I would ease myself up onto my elbow and with my eyes squinted peek through the opening of the screen and imagine that I was dancing with them until I couldn't keep my eyes open a minute longer. I always slept like a baby in my Nana's house because it felt like heaven – whatever and wherever that was. So, when my Nana died back then from colon cancer, and according to those religious lies, was a sinner and would be damned to hell, I cursed God and damned him to hell and the inner rebellion began.

The first visible sign of that inner rebellion manifested in my body as painful hives that would viciously attack my eyes, lips, tongue, and feet leaving me grotesquely deformed and incapacitated for several days at a time. No itching, just a painfully swelling and aching disability that seemed to come out of nowhere and force me into a fetal position on lockdown hidden away from other's eyesight in my parents' bedroom and bed. My mother would try to soothe my swollen body parts with witch hazel and comfort my tortured mind with affirmations that there was nothing too hard or complex that God could not and would not heal. My father would often surprise me with his signature meal – spaghetti and meatballs, which I could never turn down even with a swollen tongue and lips. But over the course of two years or so these hives became more and more relentless. I didn't realize until much later in life that this was how I got my nurturing and loving attention from mom and dad. Mom would hold me against her chest and dad would cook for me and tell me scary stories.

But the hives continued and finally, my parents took me to a doctor and after running every allergy test imaginable, entered the verdict that my disfiguring hives were the result of "stress" – period. My father sighed and my mother, in spiritually flossed language, told the doctor to go to hell and that there was nothing too hard for God. Stress – what the hell was stress? Well, whatever it was or wasn't, it rendered me more and more angry, confused and needing to keep my imaginary world alive, vibrant and sustainable because the day to day obviously was too stressful.

To support that ever-increasing desire, I began reading love stories and watching movies over and over again starring Rita Hayworth, Joan Crawford and especially Betty Davis's, "All This and Heaven Too", every chance I could get. The dramatic characters they portrayed and the love stories behind, around and in front of these characters fed and nurtured something so deep inside of me that I began to welcome the opportunity to stay home from school more days than I needed to because of my hives.

My imagination became entangled in a web of illusions and delusions laced with seductively daunting images of our epic Queens BaSheba and Cleopatra lulling my body into an aching, burning desire to reconnect to the splendor of divine union with my heavenly king like I saw on the screen. Where on earth was this stuff coming from at such a ripe and tender age?

Not only did my imagination go through the roof, but I began to write my own 12-year-old's take on dramatic, vivid and intricate romance short stories with adult characters that detailed subject matter that I had not been privy to in this lifetime, enthralled with the idea of love. I also began to spew poetically heated ramblings that challenged what was "supposed" to be, out from my soul like someone who had been on this earth plane much longer than I had. I would spend hours entertaining myself propped up on my dresser, which was my imaginary piano, and in front of my imaginary audience and belt out Billy Holiday and Etta James ballads. I can see myself like it was yesterday, sipping on Kool aide from my vintage Flintstone cartoon glassware pretending that it was whiskey and puffing on my Crayola crayon cigarette motioning to my piano player to play it one more time.

And, then one day I realized, the hives were gone – only to be replaced years later with fibroid tumors again and again.

Trying to be perfectly enough

During my teenage years, I believe, is when I really lost myself in trying to find myself. Who I was trying to be, I was not. Serendipitously, my mother (with her hand on her hip and a glare in her eyes) had an incessant need to ask me, "Girl, do you know who you are?"

I knew I was Robin Scott, but I also knew it was a trick question. I would look at her as if to say, "No ma'am, I don't."

Inevitably the answer would be, "You are a Scott!" And then she would briskly walk away, annoyed that I still didn't know, or for the 1,000th time had forgotten.

Well, it took me many years to figure out what it meant to her to be a Scott, and, eventually, what it really meant for me. Back then, what I knew about who I was, was that I was too good to be bad and too bad to be good, especially as Reverend and Missionary "Scott's" daughter.

As a "too bad to be good young teenager", I got involved with Mr. Dangerous, a man 10 years older than I. This was a bold and dangerous step in trying to find out and prove who I was and the consequences proved to be equally as dangerous.

Adolescence can be such a distorted time because you think you're grown; however, you don't have the maturity and cognitive reasoning of a real grown up. Therefore, the decisions made are often from a juvenile, in the moment, state of mind with a flippant F--- the consequences attitude. And those consequences weighed quite heavily in the moment and down the road.

So, when I became pregnant at age 16, my beautiful imagination desperately wanted to craft a grand story about an immaculate conception to present to my parents. Even though I had a certain idea that no matter how much my mother believed in Mary, Joseph and her immaculate conception of Jesus born in a manger, that story was not going to fly about how who was growing inside of me got inside of me.

As grown as I believed I was, there was nothing that came from my 16-year-old mouth that could prevent the inevitable and part of the inevitable was that Mr. Dangerous, prior to knowing that I was pregnant, committed a very serious crime that resulted in him going to prison.

What had I gotten myself into and who had I gotten myself involved with? My mind was spinning and I was a pregnant teenager. This sealed the decision my parents were going to make anyway, and at 16 weeks pregnant, I was forced to abort my baby and told what a disappointment I was to my family and above all, God.

The experience was so surreal and laid the groundwork for me to begin my unconscious detachment from my womb and my heart. From the time the decision was made that I couldn't keep my baby to when I entered that hospital, no one cared to ask me how I was feeling or doing. It was as if there was a pre-agreed upon vow of silence.

I laid in the hospital bed for two days trying to journal, trying to release these ancient yet familiar silent screams that couldn't even make it onto the paper. Instead, I was shut down in the hospital bed, hooked up to an intravenous bag that dripped a thunderously sounding poisonous substance into my body to slowly annihilate and then rapidly expel this innocent life out of my womb. During this excruciating experience, the nurse held my hand, while I stared into her eyes and silently screamed again and again. After the machine stopped extracting my daughter from within me, I asked her if it was a girl?

She turned away from me and said, "I'm so sorry. I can't answer that question."

"No problem," I said. Somehow, I already knew they'd just killed my baby girl.

When my parents picked me up from the hospital, it was clear that what had taken place during those three days was never to be spoken about – and we didn't. At that time, I couldn't forgive either of them for orchestrating the brutal abortion of my first child, expelled from my young, yet ancient womb. Back home inside my room, I wept for what seemed like centuries. This pain felt very old and heavy, so I decided to sing, dance, and swing my hips to a different drum and write it all away.

You see, I desperately wanted to be free. I felt trapped in somebody else's world. Over the next year, I concocted a ridiculously rebellious plan to drop out of high school, turn my part time job into full time and escape from my parent's religious prison barracks for good. My newfound hippie flower child values flavored with a budding revolutionary Black power uprising "power to the people" manifesto had me standing firm with this plan.

When my mother realized that I was not backing down, she insisted that my father bring me to my senses by any means necessary. And he did. For the first time that I could remember, he spoke to me like a dad who really cared about

ME.

I mean, I knew within me that, yes, daddy loved me, because that's what daddies are supposed to do. But, until this moment, he was either at work, sleeping, preaching, and carrying so much heavy weight that caused him to literally gain a whole lot of physical weight, which challenged his health.

When we sat down to really talk, he asked me what had prompted this decision and if I would be open to hearing some other options. Wow, my heart began to open like a thirsty flower. We communed about my future for days like a loving daughter and father and finally, he begged me to push on through and graduate in May of the following year.

His final words to me on this matter were, "Please, if this still doesn't make sense to you Robin, then do it for me – do it for me." With tears in my eyes, I hugged him and agreed that I would graduate for him.

In April of the following year, just one month before my graduation, my dad died suddenly at home in his bedroom from his 6th heart attack. I still remember seeing him on the floor with his eyes open, the empty vanilla and strawberry ice cream container that he wasn't supposed to be eating and a look of peace on his face, anyway. His death startled me, and unfortunately, further alienated me from my mother at a time soon before I was to become a mother – yup again. She demanded that the paramedics must not stop working on him, even though they said he was gone. I stood on our staircase landing between my father still upstairs and my mother downstairs in the church affirming that God would intervene… but he didn't this time. I was terrified when they started bringing him downstairs and smiling simultaneously, as I looked at his slightly greying face. Looking at him, I began remembering the scary stories he would tell me and my sister, when we were little about how dead people looked, as he would make these dead people ghostly noises and chase us around the house.

Wow, viewing his dead face forced me to remember those playful dead folks' horror stories from my daddy. I could also see his bare foot, dangling on the side of the stretcher, and remembered mom washing his stinky feet and then anointing them with her holy oil. My sister and I thought that was disgusting. But mom would say, "You must always treat your husband as a King." Then she would smile, and wink her eye saying, "and he must know that you are a Queen."

Before the paramedics could take him out into the ambulance, my mother who was intensely quoting biblical scriptures, told them to stop as she walked over to him and affirmed that, "This is not the end Bob; this is not the end." The following month, suffering from a deep sense of abandonment because it was the end, I kept my word and graduated just for him and that brought me a little speck of peace.

Moving into the next year was a haze filled mist of reckless behavior and finally, as the dust began to fade, a young woman who needed to feel lovable and loving began to emerge. I loved hanging out in Harvard Square. The prestigious and world-renowned university think tanks – Harvard and Radcliff – were strategically placed to accommodate an eclectic blend of different cultures from around the world, most importantly to me at that time, Africa. As a confirmed Afro wearing free styling hippie, I loved hanging out in the Cambridge coffee houses at night meeting a whole new world of people from around the world. Then, the piece de resistance was dancing to African drumming as an unencumbered revolutionary sistah like clockwork every Sunday afternoon in the Cambridge commons.

This seemingly dichotomy of prestige, intellect and free styling soul stirring multiculturalism was a reflection of the conflict that I was struggling to resolve within my spirit. Do you know who you are – and how-to live-in alignment with that knowing? No! But I was trying to figure that out. Up until that point in my life, I never figured that Africa would play a part in that knowing, and even more importantly, Ethiopia. The same country I remembered hearing my father preach on in one of his soulful sermons; that Ethiopia shall rise again. Now, even though I wasn't into the bible, this time it grabbed me – stuck in my memory and stuck within me.

I could feel that love was in the air. As I began to intuitively breathe that in, I knew he would join me in co-creating the next stage of my life. Tall, deliciously dark, and very handsome, I met him in one of those coffee houses and he was from Ethiopia – go figure. But my spirit knew his spirit like he had always lived just around the corner. He spoke to my heart in a language of love that needed no translation, and I knew that we would be linked in this life – so – I – thought, forever.

For the first time, since I had my heart-to-heart conversation with my father, I began to feel the warmth and glow of love and my heart began to welcome that much needed feeling of aliveness again. His passion for life was in full throttle and ignited a hunger within me for something bigger and greater than me that I didn't know existed before. Although, I must admit that once again trying to keep up with someone else's bigger than life worldview began to diminish the view of me from my own big brown eyes. Over time, my old views of not being enough began to tarnish this new vision that went beyond Harvard Square or Boston. This spread throughout the world. I began to struggle with the thoughts of how I could keep up with this man who was a walking and talking genius. This felt so familiar and old at the same time. After several months, our love grew and my belly also began to grow with a baby that I knew no matter what my mother thought, I was going to birth.

Even though, I was eighteen, once again, my mother was shocked and devastated because my union with Mr. Ethiopia fell under God's law of fornication, and the only way to reconcile this sin – again – against God she said, was to stand before him and 100 church folks and take a vow of marriage. "Hell, NO!" was my first response. I mean who is this God? And what is it that I owe him? This was a question that - little did I know - would be haunting me for a while. It was like some kind of debt, or something that you are called to pay this property owner that I had to please.

"Your God does not define who I am!", I blurted out! I was not going to let my mother and her God tell me that I was going to have another abortion because I'd sinned against him. This time around, no matter what, I was going to be in control of my own womb.

Then, to my surprise, my mother and I began to find some common ground. Wow! Not knowing who I was trying to impress, or what I was repressing I said, "yes" to the church wedding. I realized that my saying yes was not to God, my saying yes was making this commitment to Mr. Ethiopia by any means necessary. However, Mr. Ethiopia said "yes" and that we needed to blend his culture into this ceremony, so that it would reflect both our worlds.

At the close of my mother's orchestrated church wedding, we were both adorned with beautiful Ethiopian fabric, while we chanted to the call and response songs and danced to the African drums. So, help me, every ounce of that ceremony felt a little more like a tapestry of me. It felt like I was not only becoming wedded to Mr. Ethiopia, and growing our son in my belly, I was also getting a stronger glimpse, taste, and smell of Mother Africa. In re-honoring my heart and womb, I thought Mr. Ethiopia and I were going to live together happily ever after forever.

Nope! No such thing; a year and a half later that union came to an end. And it left me with the opportunity to struggle and stretch with the euphemism that relationships are for a reason, season, or lifetime. My marriage and vows proved to be for a reason and a very short season that would help me to begin to better understand my journey into my core wounds of "not being good enough and abandonment". However, I was blessed with a son, destined to carry on Mr. Ethiopia and my daddy's earlier sermon, which I still remember to this day, Ethiopia shall rise again.

Here I was a single mom now living across the street from my mom and trying to figure out what's next. It certainly was a very difficult time, and it was a time for me to start thinking about me. "Come on girl; get it together." Well with a baby in my arms and the realization that this responsibility was going to be primarily in my hands, I really had to focus on what the future could and needed to look like.

As I began to process all the messed-upness that I had been witnessing from all those superficial love stories and why we do the things that we do; that curiosity guided me to explore psychology – hmmm. Do you know who you are? I heard my mother's voice echoing in my head and my dad talking about the major importance of education. Well, I was starting to figure out a little bit more of who I could be... maybe, you think? Perhaps, I'm someone who can help someone start rewriting their own life story. But that meant I had better start rewriting mine. I began to ask myself, what can my life begin to really look like through my own big brown eyes?

So off to college I went, majoring in psychology and about a year later life was starting to feel and look a little better, until Mr. Dangerous was released from jail. His attempt at trying to reconnect with me was terrifying and the threats he made, I believed could really happen, and I had no clue as to how to protect myself. Yes, I felt helpless, vulnerable, and scared for my baby and this sent me to the police department demanding help. To my surprise, Officer Protector stepped in on my behalf like a warrior and told Mr. Dangerous, if I so much as got a mosquito bite, look out.

Was I really good enough for this level of protection? You're doggone right, I was! So, I tried again, even though things were a little messy, now with Officer Protector. This handsome smooth talking powerful, kickass man stepped up and stepped in. And four years later, sure enough, my belly began to rise again with my second son. However, like I said, it was messy and after eight years that journey ended as well, leaving me with another amazing son also destined to protect, maintain and provide. Mr. Dangerous and Officer Protector helped me to fully see from my big brown eyes that whether you are the victim and/or the perpetrator, each and all are seeing and telling their story from their fragmented side of the "truth".

Chapter Two
~ Collecting My Soul's Threads ~

In the years that followed, my two sons blessed and stretched my life. It was much more challenging being a single mother raising two brilliant and curious minded sons in the heart of the urban community back in the late 1980s and early 1990s. I must admit that living across the street from my mother and her church was helpful and challenging at the same time. As grandma to my sons, she was to them - in many ways - what my Nana had been to me. She loved her grandsons unconditionally and supported me in every way possible as a single mom. However, she still felt like following her pathway to God was what I needed in my life. "Hell to the no!" I silently screamed in her ears, as I diligently sought out spiritual paths that were more in alignment with my truth.

My life had become a magical multifaceted kaleidoscope, reflecting the spiritual and everyday multidimensional aspects of myself as a devoted mother, ardent college student and, to top it all off, a drop dead awesome high fashion runway model. That's correct; I spent many years starting in the late 1970s in the fashion industry consumed with focusing on the artificially glamorous aspects of myself, along with an Image Consulting business to boot. Talk about fragmented pieces, all my cues and clues about who I was were driven by a society and an industry that thrived on faking it until you make it and looking good even if you don't. Whew, and by the way, did I mention that I was also making the world a better place as a devotee of AMWAY the top "network marketing" business in the country at that time? Yes, I was.

I was acting out roles on live stages that dealt with everything from HIV, gang violence and unfulfilled love stories, while actively out in the world identifying myself as an "African American Revolutionary Evolutionary", destined to transform an oppressive world system. Wow, it was all me! Passion was the fuel that catapulted me along some of the finest runways to the revolutionary shores of "Black Nationalism" fighting for the rights of my oppressed and disenfranchised sisters and brothers. "Power to the People" was my melodic chant. Those shores later carried me down the path of the Nation of Islam's powerful do for self-teachings of the Honorable Elijah Muhammad and Minister Louis Farrakhan.

While in grad school, studying for my master's degree in counseling, I came across a startling statistic stating that 50% of the women killed in the United States were murdered by their husband or boyfriend. That statistic compelled me to write my first screenplay (later adapted for stage) called *And I Love You Richard* as my thesis, while doing my internship at Renewal House, a transformational shelter for women survivors of domestic abuse, which I later became the director of for several years.

After grad school that insatiable passion was also channeled as a rebellious non-traditional psychotherapist fighting fiercely for the rights of battered and disempowered women, Black folks and the homeless, while now zigzagging over the yellow brick road into the spiritual Buddhist tradition, with a zealously new chant called "nam myoho ren ga kyo" which is a sacred vow to yourself to never yield into your difficulties so that you can overcome all obstacles for oneself and others. Oh yeah, and my connection to the Afro-Cuban spiritual tradition of Santeria and the spiritual practices I learned from my Padrino (spiritual guide) is what helped me to avoid danger zones for my sons in their teenage years. Dang! I really did all of that.

And yet, with all that I was doing on the outside, it still wasn't enough. I began envisioning myself as this "Revolutionary Evolutionary" star being interviewed by Johnny Carson on his late-night TV show talking about the success of my latest movie Oh, and let's not forget the Academy and Tony awards that I just knew I was going to win along with another bestselling new book I had written. I don't know where these fantasies were coming from, but they were so vivid and sometimes it would make me feel like I was crazy. I mean come on, what am I really longing for and who am I… really?

Okay, I was doing pretty good acting on those stages, walking up and down runways, writing and, being a "Revolutionary Evolutionary" while chanting. Well maybe not of the magnitude that I was envisioning on the outside.

Nevertheless, the more I began to reassess my own stage dramas some different stage lights were starting to shine on me, and I noticed that I had a real and tangible revolutionary blueprint to evolve. The need for this blueprint was connected to what I was seeing with some of the models and actors that I personally was connected to or from listening to the news about the major stars in Hollywood.

I realized that many of them were suffering no matter how much they were getting paid; the price they had to pay to maintain their fame and fortune was breaking their hearts. And far too many had shut down and were not even in tune to the pain and suffering they were living behind the scenes.

I realized that many of these folks that I personally knew had been coming to me with their pain and suffering because they knew something about me that I had yet to know. As I began to get out of my bigger than life award winning star fantasies, I started recognizing that maybe I was already a "natural" healer. Wow! Well, this became the conscious beginning of my own healing process from the inside out. Yup, I asked myself what I was really looking for and again did I really know who I was? What was my true story and was I ready to really rewrite, edit and live out who I "really" am on the "real" stage called life? This realization drew me into using my gift for poetry and short story writing to re-form how I needed to transform my personal and societal pain. I was also beginning the formal process to become a holistic therapist. I strongly believed that I needed to bridge my artistic work and my activism into a "Healing Through the Arts" evolutionary means for transforming internalized pain, suffering and imposed injustices from the "Inside Out".

See, I was hungry for something… sensually and passionately fulfilling. All these revolutionary evolutionary, psychological, spiritual, and artistic practices were nourishing the safety net container that I was living inside of at that time. I knew I was ready to release all the sterile outside bird's-eye view of the external psychological trappings that sidetrack and distract our insatiable minds.

From somewhere above and beyond me I was desperately seeking to know who I really was once and for all from the true inside of me. Not the cellophane roles I was repeatedly playing on and off the theater stages and runways. Physically, mentally, and emotionally exhausted, and in a state of total surrender I began silently screaming, who am I?

As I began to scream this deeper more penetrating question about my personal role, also known as purpose, here on Earth, the truth about our *collective* human purpose and of course, who and what role does this Universal creator (also known as Father God that I damned to hell) play? Sure enough, I began hearing faint whispers echoing from somewhere deep within me and around me. Soon the whispering voices became piercingly thunderous like those silent screams within me.

"STOP!!!!! Please," I begged. "Stop screaming! Please! I can't hear you when you scream!"

The raspy bodacious roar of this voice was deafening. It bellowed throughout my inner sanctum like a whispered echo riding on a frequency familiar – yet way too far away to comprehend. This was a primordial tone: rich, pulsating, sound vibrating. Older than old, it was Ancient. It was what would become, for me, a whole different knowing of God, and it was "Feminine".

This was an ancient new knowing for me. And, in the early stages of hearing these voices, I was somewhat scared. And yes, scared or not, I needed to know more about who I am. Not just a Scott. I was ready to "experience the truth" about my divine essence – to remember who I really am. And be careful what you ask for because within a flash of light my body began to tremble, and I heard, felt, and fully experienced the echoed whispers of who I later remembered were "The Ancient Mothers".

> *...my sister, do you know who you really are? Do you really know? Are you willing to look beyond the veil of illusion into the portal of your own ancient wisdom and reenact your divine herstory? Do you remember from whence you originated? Do you remember what your authentic cellular essence is made from? Do you remember how far back or forward the umbilical cord of your magnetic feminine soul reaches and stretches? Can you remember resting deep within the primordial fluid inside the "Cosmic Womb of **The Great Mother**"?*

Oh, my goodness!!! Who's womb? And cosmic! Well, I asked for it and there was no turning these voices down or off. As I surrendered my mind and body, they ushered me into what I later began to understand through my deep meditation, yoga and breathwork practices, that I was moving into higher levels of conscious awareness. As I listened more intently, I felt myself ascending and transcending into what's called the "Akashic Records" which gives us conscious access to "The All Knowing – The Absolute" that we are all interconnected to. In many non-dogmatic spiritual traditions this is known as the inner dimensions of our higher self. It's also referred to as the "Etheric Living Library" and the Higher Dimensions of our Planetary Earth Mother.

Wow! While within this higher space of deeper awareness, I began to slowly remember and see these fragmented pieces of my soul, not only from this lifetime, but from infinity. It was like being in a movie theater watching these trailers of many different lifetimes of ME on this big screen.

There, within the realm of the infinite, the eternal, I started to uncover the uniquely different puzzle pieces from many of my lifetimes. I began to realize that the SOUL is the divine infinite essence of consciousness that incarnates through the breath into the human vessel known as the physical body.

The knowledge of my soul's journey that was being revealed is that it is primarily for the divine purpose of expression and experience, and then returns to its omniversal state of consciousness when the physical body expires/death. Consciously accessing and reconnecting to many of the pertinent roles that my soul has engaged in over many different lifetimes and the repeated challenges within those lifetimes were now illuminating the fragmented pieces of my journey home to "Absolute Wholeness" as a glimpse of my evolving self. I realized that many of my major lifetimes carried a consistent theme that was being played out in this lifetime, and that these lifetimes were just the multicolored clothing of "**The Great Mother** – the Feminine aspect of what we call "God" that adorned my soul.

What I came to realize over time, after that experience and through some of the deep experiential "inner child" work I was doing within my theater group called "Up from Silence", is that we are not our stories. The entire play that our soul is engaging in is a series of chapters, acts, and scenes in "The Book of Life".

> *All our karmic lessons are personally selected, specifically to aid us in the various areas of self-mastery and ultimately back*

> *home to spiritual perfection. As we individually and collectively remember our multidimensional beingness, we're able to transcend our 3rd dimensional earthly mundane reality with all its emotional baggage and traumas.*

Wow and bang! Something began to shift within me, and with a delicate freshly blooming awareness, I realized I was being called to look deep within and give myself permission to take my search into the depths of my evolving self and weave the "Tapestry of My Soul's" journey into a sensual perfectly imperfect mosaic of ART.

As I went on to master my karmic lessons this exploration took me deeper and deeper inside the inside of me and the true essence of my personal love story. I was certainly planning to rewrite my story this time with my "Cosmic Beloved" as my co-leading character. Now where was that coming from?

Chapter Three
~ My Introduction to Sacred Sexuality ~

My early sexual experiences, like for so many women, served as a kinesthetic means of fulfilling, at that time, what I believed was loving intimate connection. However, all of that began to shift dramatically in the late eighties and early nineties when my intellectual search for higher spiritual truth began to guide my spirit even deeper into the spiritual traditions of Buddhism, Sufism, Tantra, Hatha Yoga, and Tibetan Reiki hands on healing, all of which were beautifully interwoven into my passion for theater, healing, and the arts.

Who were those men,
men that I
came to know
in the shadows of my heart
gentle kisses
hearts yearning
passion burning
in the blazing sun
were they really there?
Innocence
unveiled
commitments failed
dishonesty revealed
did they
really, really
care?

Buddhism gave me a panoramic glimpse into the world of

meditation and breathed life into the concept that all of us are – already "Divine Beings". This was major for me. My introduction into Sufism was through the renowned Sufi poet Rumi. His deliciously delirious renditions of the "Beloved" ushered me into the rapture of the divine. This was a breakthrough because my relationship with God, as you read earlier, had been consciously severed in my early childhood when my nana, who wasn't Pentecostal, died and the dogmatically interpreted teachings of the bible surely damned her soul to hell. After that traumatic loss, YUP, I cursed God and damned his soul to hell... remember?

Now, Tantra, was the cosmic loom that embraced all the universal remnants within creation (like me) and weaved them into a harmonious web/tapestry. Through the Tantric lens all is one and that cosmic oneness can be accessed, experienced, and manifested through the sensory body and anchored into this physical mundane reality. Reiki gave me the hands-on energy healing skill set for healing and transforming this mundane reality. Tantra also guided me into understanding Kundalini "sacred sexual" lifeforce energy that when activated through our chakras guides you into the higher realms of consciousness, also known as ascension. And of course, Hatha Yoga is about Union and the purification of mind, body, and spirit in preparation for that Union so that we are better equipped to live in alignment with these higher universal truths – but of course I didn't know any of that then.

During this time, I began to have an intense longing to go *home* I wanted to return to a place that clearly was not my earthly residence and was also not in Boston. I hated Boston and all the heinous historical documentation of the laws enforced to retain and maintain the abuse of my enslaved Africa, African American and Native American ancestors which New England/Boston proudly heralded. I so did not belong in this city and sometimes I would awaken in the middle of the night sobbing and longing to return to my real home that seemed so far away, and yet somewhere inside of me, I knew was as close as my fingertips. Yet, I didn't have a clue as to how to get there. It was a deep longing – much like the ET character that was so homesick and longed to return to his home in the stars.

I had no idea at the time that all of this longing for home, my spiritual fire awakening, the experiential theater work I was involved in – oh yeah – and the energy healing work I was doing was consciously and unconsciously designed to help me deal with my unresolved masculine abandonment issues regarding my father and my sons' daddies. I would soon see that the rebirthing breath work, I had stumbled upon, was going to greatly revolutionize my understanding of the true power associated with the sacred sexual energy in preparation for planting my feet on the path of the African Goddess Orisa Osun – more about her later.

You see this longing for home began to mimic a pulsating sensation that I was feeling in my heart for a closeness that I just couldn't put my finger on, nor could I expect from future relationships. I was looking for something deeper, higher, much more organic, and authentic than what I had been experiencing. Yet I had no clue as to where this longing was coming from or taking me to – until two incredible life changing experiences surfaced.

The first one happened during a rebirthing breath session I was having. Rebirthing is a powerful healing tool that involves continuous open mouth circular breathing patterns that can transport you into the bowels of your emotional body. I had experienced several cathartic individual breath sessions with a trained rebirthing facilitator.

After running out of money and thinking I had to end my private sessions, she suggested I attend their less expensive weekly group sessions. So, I did, and what I experienced during that first session was life transforming and affirming. Once I was able to get over the awkwardness, fear, and vulnerability of doing this very personal work within a group of strangers, I began to feel a cocoon of safety being woven all around me and soon I sensed myself slipping inside the inside of the inside of my body.

Inside this awareness I soon began to sense these incredible pulsating waves that seemed to have their origin somewhere in the core of my body. This motion was subtle initially, and then intensified with my deeper levels of breathing and body awareness. My brain could not fathom these waves of sensation, but my body knew them well. You see up to that point in my life I had never experienced (real) sexual orgasms.

Like so many women I didn't know how to, and, like in the movies, had been faking them all the time. Now when the real deal was happening in a room full of people (all in their own worlds of course) I was awestruck. I also heard myself speaking in some other language. Now, that was even more breathtaking. I didn't know what these sounds or words were. All I knew was that it also felt familiar and had some kind of audible vibration that totally encapsulated me… all of me.

How did my body know how to do this all by herself??? What was the impetus for this??? Where is this coming from and how do I do it again??? These were the questions my brain was begging my body to explain. And as those thoughts began to intrude on my level of body awareness, a slither of pain so deep and so sharp began to penetrate and almost obliterate my ecstasy. Within a matter of seconds, some way and somehow, I began to comprehend that my ability to have sexual orgasm had been circumvented by some kind of unconscious sexually painful experiences embedded within my womb. But the gateway to ecstasy was now open and despite the pain I did not want that door to close.

Wow! It Gets Better Than This?!

This was a journey I was fervently committed to explore. Perhaps a year later, I was ushered into my first other lifetime altering experience and remembrance. I was laying on the massage table receiving a Reiki energy healing session from one of my male colleagues whom I often exchanged healing sessions with. We had been working on releasing the armor around my belly area also known as the sacral chakra. There was something that continued to block the brief melodious ecstasy that I had become privy to during that erotic breath work session. As he began energetically tuning in to my womb area, I was beginning to feel the release melting away what felt like lifetimes of antiquated beliefs, values and conditionings encased within this frozen block inside my womb. Breathing deeply and fully I began to surrender to that now familiar place and slipped into that ancient abyss that resides between now and infinity. And I was catapulted home, finally – yes home. And I started to ascend and remember…

> …And within the blink of a thousand eyes, my soul just started to remember. Remember a time beyond before. A time that feels like time and space ceased to exist - a time so indescribable. How do I describe something so incredibly indescribable? A memory of something that is so deeply subtle, expansively profound, massively multidimensional, and yet, so intricately personal that it starkly penetrates the multi-layers of my existence. Something so gently earth shattering that it shakes away all traces of the illusions of this world that are retained within my soul's cellular memory. How do I describe something so vital and so instinctually primal welling up from the deepest part of my core? And with mountainous wings, wrapping my essence into a multicolored tapestry of overflowing reams and reams and reams of love?
>
> Memories of something so enchantingly soothing enveloping my heart and rocking my spirit into an ancient abyss of blissful knowing. A knowing that I am encased within my own stellar being experiencing the cosmos stretching before and beyond me in perfect harmony. That day my soul opened, and I began to remember that indescribable state of grace

surrounding me as I sensuously sensed the pulsing urge from my divine creative knowing for yet another creation. The seductive waves of creation penetrated my being, and I grew thirsty with sheer delight to begin a lusciously new adventure.

I remember experiencing atoms exploding into a quiet symphony of sound. Radiant and luminous colors of stillness undulated throughout the vulva of my consciousness as I co-created our heaven, sun, stars, the moon, and all that exist within the higher realms from within the sacred nectar of my womb. And I knew the I AM and that I Am One with the All. That was the first time I consciously remembered knowing Who I Am.

And, then I remember nature thrusting us into the epitome of earthly descent. Spiraling effortlessly through a luminous tube in a downward motion away from the vast Oneness of All that my heart still yearns for – home – the illuminating star of the white sand. Our journey began there, in the Sanctuary with us close, so very close. I could feel you so close. It's as if you were my "breath". It was awesome. Feeling the singular motion of our One breath propelling me out from the rapture of infinity into the illusion of separate, but still one. I don't even dare to remember us separate, only close, only One. We were in the same cell, the same body, no, the same essential essence of whispering vapors. Yes, that's what it was. We were the same cell, the same molecular atom of timeless bliss. Wow! We were so close. I can smell you and taste you in the saliva of my mind. The smell was fragrantly masculine and the taste deliciously feminine. Misty, wet, full, gently full, firm, and open. Motion. Continuous motion.

It is all there. All the stellar, omniversal and genetic coding is there. We Are **The Perfect Sacred Union**. And out from the memory of our One consciousness, we energetically divided ourselves to reproduce our divine essence throughout the entire universe in co-creation of the duality of humanity. We lay embraced in naked innocence intertwined in effortless love making without movement, without thought, filled with the

> *stillness of joy, intimate bliss, and total surrender. The Oneness of our breath rising and fading like newborn waves riding on a gentle breeze in the summer rain, nestling us deeply into the remembrance of our origin. Allowing us within the grace of that divine knowing to subtly and powerfully merge "energetically" and reproduce All of creation over and over again from our sacred essence. And in a breathless moment birthed from the womb of infinity, we're split into the illusion of night or day. Up, down. Left and right. Feminine, masculine, black and white. Wrong and right. Animal, mineral, hot, cold, them and us. You and me. Separate, alone, and lifetime after lifetime in search of reunion with the Oneness of Creation.*

That was the first time that I knew that the longing for home and the heart pounding desire to re-connect was my innate desire to return to the stellar home within. From deep inside the inside of me I now knew that my sacred reunion with my Beloved Twin Soul was what I had been longing for during this lifetime. I was being guided back into the cosmic origin of me as One even before US. Now that I was remembering this heartfelt remembrance, hopefully, our earthly reunion would begin again… Please.

Yeah, But There Was Something Still Festering Within My Womb

That session was an amazing reentry into me, and all of this was good, and not so good. You see I began to really ponder about this Beloved, and the more I pondered I began to feel deep within my womb… the unresolved RAGE connected to this ancient core wound of abandonment and not being good enough simmering in a pool of grief that I thought no longer existed.

> *The simmering is over*
> *The tiny glistening bubbles*
> *Are transforming*

> *Into blazing, grotesque images.*
> *Loomingly dashing in and out*
> *With fanged teeth*
> *And fierce tongues.*
> *Stark faces and huge talking heads.*
> *Demons clamor to be FREE*
> *Set in motion*
> *By just the thought*
> *Of being*
> *Me*

I was grieving some kind of ancient sadness that was permeating inside my womb… grieving the empty spaces within my heart… grieving the loss of my power… grieving what seemed like lifetimes of unexpressed volcanic rage for the violations, desecrations and the vicious torturing of my womb and the wombs of my African, Cherokee, African American and European "Ancient Ancestral Mothers".

But how did I know this Grieving Rage?

I began to realize that so much of this unresolved anger and simmering rage with my mother and father had far less to do with the physical forms of them and the parental roles they played in my life this time around.

You see how they saw me as perhaps precocious and yet not Godly enough, set the stage for this challenging journey of my partnered relationships, and all the misconstrued and misunderstood rights and wrongs. So, my struggle with my natural sensual nature and how I was needing to be loved, what was a good girl and a bad woman, and all the inner turmoil began to fester and ignite blisters of rage that ultimately showed themselves within my womb as fibroid tumors.

At a time when I thought I was in the right zone, paying closer attention to my choices and choosing to support women day and night at Renewal House, a domestic violence shelter, I still had not gone deep enough. I was dealing with repeated yeast and urinary tract infections along with an unquenched desire for my Beloved that made me keep looking for love outside of me.

Fortunately, just in time to save my womb from another violent extraction, I was introduced to a very special gynecologist who would help me on the medical side begin gaining greater insight into the intricacies of my womb. During a regular GYN visit, to my surprise he said, "You have the beginning of what, if not handled properly, could turn into a cyst inside your vaginal cavity."

I was stunned and curious at the same time.

He paused for a moment noticing the look on my face as I struggled to understand what the word cyst meant. With a caring smile on his face, he stood up covered my sacred area, and retrieved some inner vaginal images from within the drawer for me to look at. With an authentically caring voice said, "Would you like to see inside your vaginal space so you will know what your healthy and unhealthy walls look like?"

What the…?! Isn't that why I'm coming to you? Isn't that your job and responsibility I thought to myself as I said, with an annoyed smile on my face, "Sure, okay."

And in a sacred format with a stethoscope inside of me and a light shining, he handed me a mirror so that I could see both sides of my inner self. The beginning of a cyst was forming on one side and the other side was plump pink and glowing.

I didn't know whether to be grateful at first or repulsed. This was the first time I was seeing inside of me. But over time I felt nothing but gratitude.

On my return visit the following year the cyst was fading but what was revealed now was the beginning of fibroid tumors.

And fortunately having a male gynecologist who valued helping women to heal and retain their sacred wombs at that time was phenomenal.

However, with all the holistic healing practices I was trying to engage in, the fibroids were growing rapidly, and the simmering rage was evidently still trapped underground. In order to prevent any further growth, he recommended a surgical procedure that would safely remove the fibroids while leaving my womb in its rightful place. It was revealed to me after the surgery that he removed nineteen fibroids.

So, I continued delving into the traumas and powers connected to my womb. I knew that somehow and some way it was time to cleanse and purify on an even deeper level from the inside out. But I had no idea just how deep inside I needed to go to find "Me" and reclaim "Me" with or without my "Beloved". The true question was: Who was I "really" looking for?

Part TWO
Cleansing and Purifying

The Fragmented Parts of Me

WHERE AM I?

You asked me not too long ago – where are you???
Not sure yet...
I just know that I'm struggling
like a fish that's been deprived from its natural habitat – water

I'm so trying to return to myself – what I know as me
You see I'm realizing that returning to my Self – is very difficult
because my-self has been strewn across the abyss of what I knew to be me

and that former knowing of me has now been scattered everywhere
like a torn-up post card from an old lover that you loved dearly
that was a part of an old life that you can't even remember anymore.

There are pieces and parts of me that I don't even know
that I've lost – misplaced – or maybe never had.
Where do you look for the most intimate aspects of you???
Where do you find the treasures that you have hidden from the world,

and even more importantly from yourself???
Treasures so deeply buried in your unconscious psyche
that to find them requires unearthing your entire sense of being.

I'm looking – however
So, know that I have started my search again.

For the first half of my life, I was in search of what some call God – now...

I am in search of my true Self which is – God
So, I'm sure that when I find God, I will find me.
And if by chance I find me first
I'm certain that I will have found God as well.

Chapter Four
~ Osun, African Tantric Goddess ~

Okay, tumors gone, and I had a mystically profound out – of – body experience. Now what? You would think that the universe opening, pulling me in, and metaphorically showing me who I was would have been enough incentive for me to begin adorning myself in white flowing robes, chanting in that strange native tongue that I had begun speaking in and raising the dead. Well in many ways I did. I mean I didn't raise any dead, at least not physically dead, but I began to take my work as a healer much more seriously and my cosmic experience brought me closer to the reality of who I was, am, or better said was to grow into. However, in far too many other ways I felt as though I was even further away from myself because with all that I had come to know – my life, my heart, and my womb – were still empty.

The residue of that experience left me with an even deeper longing to be embraced by the fullness of who I truly was and to consummate that knowing in the blissful sacred reunion with that divine energy I experienced. But how? I still didn't know the how and – the why – why me? I earnestly and urgently began to commune with whom I had come to now know as "Spirit" regarding the purpose of my incarnation, the truth about creation, how to manifest my divine purpose and give birth to who I truly AM; the spirit who incarnated in the form of this African American and Native American woman.

And now the universal paths of Sufism, Buddhism and Tantra that had been illuminating my tracks were guiding me back home to Mama Africa where these spiritual traditions have all originated from. With grace and gratitude, I landed onto the footsteps of Ifa, the West African ancient "spiritual tradition" of many Nigerian Yoruba people and the origin of Santeria and began to explore their four major pillars of truth. My feet joyfully danced while the universe began to spoon feed my hungry heart these ancient morsels of primal wisdom.

This six-thousand-year-old spiritual tradition through their sacred oracles provided all humanity with a cosmological blueprint for living in harmony with the natural forces of nature. Yes, the stars, moon, trees, the sun, the wind, the mountains, and butterflies (and I love butterflies) are all referred to as Orisa. You see in Ifa it is believed that each of these Orisa is imbued with their own Asé (consciousness or life force) and that identical Asé is also found embedded within human consciousness.

Ifa cosmology shows that these cosmic forces have a direct influence on our very existence and that our relationship to an Orisa begins even prior to our conception. Wow! I was beginning to see the tie in to so many of the other spiritual traditional paths I had been strolling along. Thus, the relationship between you and your primary Orisa are a part of your sacred incarnation agreement and living in alignment with the energy of your primary Orisa can help you to fulfill your destiny and usher you into higher states of consciousness – called home. I don't know about you, but I knew I was on the right track.

These sacred oracles hold the keys to knowing our soul's purpose. And with this knowledge, you can become attuned to the rhythm of your own drum. Ifa also gave me the sacred water pouring ritual called libations to begin strengthening the bond between me and my ancestors – stretching back seven generations and beyond. My heart soared and my head bowed in honor and reverence for our ancestors as I learned to pour libations at the altar of their souls. Then I listened to their ancient wisdom, which yielded such simple truths… for they are the wisdom keepers, and I AM because they are. I began the noble discipline of cultivating Iwa Pele/good moral character, much like nam myoho renge kyo, which is essential in walking the path of service, and to ensure that one becomes a revered elder within the human family, as well as wisdom keeper in the ancestral realm. These were very important job descriptions for humanity.

by Deniese Woolfolk

And finally, I looked into the mirror of my heart and saw the face of my Orisa, Osun – African Tantric Goddess staring back at me. Like hand in glove, this was a natural fit. Osun is one of Ifa's principal goddesses. This elemental sweet water deity is one of the most spiritually powerful of the Orisa. She is the archetypal embodiment of natural beauty, refinement, sensual flow and movement, artistic endeavor, creative imagination, and "Love". In her mythical role as leader of the **Iyaami (powerful feminine beings)**, she is honored and revered as a natural spiritual alchemist in the feminine mysteries of transmutation and manifestation. Her alluring erotic nature is the spark of passionate desire needed to attract the forces of expansion and contraction into the rhythmic dance of creation. Images of the magnetic and mystifying Osun often depict her as voluptuous, round, and curvaceous symbolizing feminine power as the seductive Creatress and the vessel of creation.

As I embraced the essence of her majestic love, the petals of my heart began to open softly and she appeared to me through the silky mist that rests upon her sweet waters, and in her melodious voice said…

> *…Sister, do you know who you really are? Do you really know? Do you really know what it means to be a woman one who gives birth to all of humanity? Sister, do you know what it means to be a feminine vessel, the sacred calabash that holds the feminine vibration of and for creation within the sanctity of your mysterious womb? Sister it is you who is the alchemical container, which holds the life giving and sustaining nectar that nourished and gave birth to the creator we have come to know as God. Oh, my dear sister, do you really know who you are? If you really want to know who you are, come to know me and let's harmoniously dance as ONE…*

I had heard this sacred voice before. So, I did. And I began consciously merging.

The Perfect Sacred Union – Many Paths One Truth

You see in nature the alluring erotic energy of Osun is experienced as the spark of desire that ignites the fires of creation into transcendence and ascension. In Tantra, Shakti the primordial feminine energy of the universe manifests as Kundalini, referenced as the sleeping serpent energy. Kundalini, like Osun, is the spark of desire that when properly awakened or aroused propels you into the realm of "Pure Consciousness" known as Shiva. Osun acts as the divine activator that attracts the spiraling polarities of expansion – Shiva and contraction – Shakti into a swirling rhythmic dance. This sacred dance is an integral ingredient in the triangular equation necessary for creation and procreation. The human ascension blueprint of this sensual essence is to elevate primal sexual expression into "Divine Spiritual Union – Home – Oneness – our pure cosmic consciousness". Wow!! This was the orgasmic energy that erupted inside my body during my rebirthing session and the blissfully erotic experience of creation I re-experienced when I was catapulted out and up into the universe during my Reiki energy healing session.

Wow, and once again I felt myself being gently catapulted back into this "Cosmic Womb". Stuttering, I asked what are you trying to tell me Osun????? Then slowly I began to spontaneously regress back into that "Perfect Sacred Union" again...

> ...Initially we didn't notice the destruction, the devolution, the madness, the rumblings, and the sadness. They were destroying it. All of it. They had everything. WE gave them everything. And they were destroying it. Then the crash came, and the earth began to rumble, roar, shake and separate. It separated. I remember seeing you on the other side. And there was so much chaos and traffic and commotion and movement and death and destruction. I couldn't find you. I couldn't see you. I couldn't feel you. I couldn't even smell you. I didn't

know where you were. That was the first time ever I felt fear, alone, lost and abandoned. Everything had changed in the twinkling of an eye. Everything. And I changed. My soul essence kept coming back over and over again, lifetime after lifetime. Looking for you. Re-experiencing the loss. I would lose my partners and my sons repeatedly to devastation and destruction. Constantly consumed and snatched away. Leaving my heart and my womb in so much pain I could barely stand it.

I could feel these ancient sensations rumbling deep inside me as I continued remembering these sensations of abandonment.

The revelation is that our very old primordial "Twin Soul" is the pure essence of God the creator. We are the original Creator Gods whose mission was to co-create humanity. We tried to avoid the harshness of earth and remain wrapped in each other's Divine Love. And we thought that we could mirror this Divine Love for humanity. Because that's what this planet was supposed to be about.

That's what we, God, were about, eternal, everlasting unconditional love. Greed destroyed the planet. Greed. Humanity wanted more and more and more and more power. It was "never enough". They became "insatiate and obnoxious". They didn't realize that it was everlasting, and they weren't going to lose it, they couldn't lose it because they were created in our image - Perfection. We were the prototype. The Elohim/Creator Gods. The Divine Love and Power were already theirs. But they got scared and didn't trust and they lost their way. They demanded more and more and more power. They abused their power. They Raped the Sacred Womb. They killed and stole and plumaged and took, and took, and took, until there was nothing left to take.

And we were so innocent, naïve. We thought they would be content just to BE (God) HU/man Beings. That's where the power comes from. BEING. The breath. So, we kept losing more and more of our Natural Self. And each time that we returned trying to recreate the innocence, passion and joy, every civilization would play out the destruction again and again, reflecting humanity's continuous fall from grace.

I began to embrace this remembrance. I began to experience a strange yet deep knowing of my purpose embodied in the deepest part of me.

> *I AM the spark to reawaken all of humanity to our Divinity. As One we procreate to recreate our Christ Self. That is the Holy Trinity. The triangle. The pyramid. The Purest and Highest feminine and masculine energies uniting in the Sacred Matrimonial Union to co-create the Holy Christ Self. This is the Immaculate Conception, and I am the Sacred Prostitute for Humanity.*

> *My body is the vessel prototype that houses the Sexual Spirit. My Womb is the spiritual vessel that brings forth gods. Yet they know not who they are. That gives birth to the Christ Spirit within. The womb is so sacred. It's the joining of the One to create the life that comes forth to save life... oh my God to give life. And humanity must come into this understanding.*

> *When we provide the right ingredients, environment, and conditions for the spiritual conception, from the womb of darkness the Christ Light of the king of kings, queen of queens, God of Gods, The Christ Self will be rebirthed as a NEW humanity.*

Oh, my goddess, did I hear her say "The Immaculate Conception" And then I began to hear the whispered echo of Osun within me silently screaming... Do you know who WE are?!

> *We are the Mothers and wives of Gods who have become the Mothers and wives of war. Holy is your name Mother of Creation. Holy is your name. Elohim, Elohim, Elohim, Elohim. Blessed be thy vessel. Blessed be thy staff. Upon entering thou must be worthy. Thou must be righteous. Thou must be cleansed by the blood. Thou must be of the Sun. Journeying from the Star of the white sand, representing life at its purest and highest.*

> *And as the Moon radiates my vulva the Sun penetrates my Being, impregnating my mind with creative ideas, inventions, and untapped potentials. Scattering my stars and creating universal light beams of Divine Love that is nourished in the genital fluids, the sacred nectar of the Gods, which aids us in impregnating and rebirthing ourselves.*

I began to joyfully scream what I was seeing, feeling, and hearing…

> *I AM the Sacred Sexual Prostitute. I AM the Sacred Virgin. I AM the Mother. I AM the daughter. I AM the Lover, the Giver, the Receiver, the Sun, and the Moon. I AM the dark in waiting of the light to penetrate my essence. Bringing forth the full expression of the universal Christ consciousness spiritually reborn from the vessel of love. Who will heed the call? I will. Elohim Amen Ra.*

Oh, my goddess! Did I really say I will heed the call as the "Sacred Sexual Prostitute"???!!! What the heck is a "Sacred Prostitute" and how can a prostitute be sacred? Fortunately, at that time through my Buddhist and Hindu tantric studies, I was coming to understand the spiraling dance of the kundalini sacred sexual energy.

As a revolutionary evolutionary I had boldly stepped into a myriad of things that stretched me near and far. The "Sacred Sexual Prostitute" and all that entailed could be a different kind of love story. However, I had to remind myself again and again that this was not some soap opera. This remembrance meant I was consciously reconnecting to the origin of my soul's essence and reliving my creation and separation from Source and my true twin flame. That experience was truly the first time that I knew that the longing for home and the heart pounding desire "to reconnect" that I had been experiencing, was my innate desire to return to the stellar home within. I began to know from somewhere within that my perfect sacred reunion with my Beloved, in human form within this lifetime, was consciously re-beginning from within.

But my imperfect self was still struggling to embrace and embody all of me.

When Perfect Still Isn't Good Enough

During my continued spiritual journey and reawakening so many wonderful things were being repeatedly revealed. However, there were parts of me that were continuing to deny the truth of what I was coming to know. I would find myself from time to time – too many times – dancing around the inability to honor these truths. Because of the lies imprinted within my true blueprint that kept me replaying some of the same distorted storylines within my "Labyrinth of Self-Circle of Life". This dissonance was greatly disturbing, and each time seemed to plunge me back into the depths of my fragmented perfectly imperfect self.

No matter what, I was determined to continue delving deeper so that I could rise higher into the true essence of me. I began to explore more consciously my own other womb lifetime stories which were within my embodied "Labyrinth of Self-Circle of Life" chart I designed. As I delved deeper, I came to realize that from within the womb of the "Cosmic Mother" and within our birth mother's womb we have complete conscious awareness of our "whole self" and all the aspects related to our wholeness. This awareness remains after birth – for a while – that is until we begin the process of separation into our individual selves.

The process of healthy separation is a part of the human experience but when we lose sight of our wholeness and begin to identify only with the distorted parts of us, we enter a life part that becomes fragmented. The vital aspects of us become lost, hidden, disconnected, repressed, disowned and unacceptable.

Thus, for many the awareness of this fragmentation and the need to consciously collect these fragmented pieces of self, ushers one into the evolutionary process of individuation. This knowledge is the inspiration to begin the journey within the "circle of life" back home to wholeness – the totality of our beingness – and that circle begins within our womb. This cyclical spiraling dance of life can also be reflected within many indigenous sacred tools such as the Labyrinth, Mandala, Medicine Wheel, Yantra, and in the West African spiritual tradition of Ifa, as the "Opon". These circles of life are also a container for our spiritual, mental, emotional, and physical self. Contained within this womb incubator are all the fragmented aspects of who we are, who we are becoming as well as the "Shadow/Illusion" that we may have of ourselves that can veil the truth of who we truly are.

In addition, each of these electromagnetic yin/yang parts of the self, have many layers – from the most subtle to the densest. In many ways the circle of life is a wheel that simultaneously encompasses all of who we are, our past, present, future reality as well as infinite possibilities. And in the center of this wheel is a dial that encompasses our conscious awareness of our whole self as well as the individual parts that make up the whole.

Our womb, which contains our sacred soul blueprint, not only holds our soul's incarnation agreements; it's also where we can begin to clear away our many lifetimes of accumulated mental and emotional toxic imprints. The accumulation of this toxicity creates an energetic film that grows into the "Shadow" self – keeping us fragmented and disconnected from our true inner self and inner knowing.

I began to realize that my toxic imprints that were distorting my true knowing and honoring of who "I Am" were playing out in a dimly lit stage spoken through a monotone, repetitive skillfully memorized script that had me wedded to the character within my own life story.

The storylines of not being feminine enough, not caring enough, not gentle enough, not supportive enough, not fair enough, not black enough, not African centered enough, too spiritual, too feminine, too maternal, too hopeful, too full of joy, trying to be enough for you, yet still not enough for you, even though I'm supposed to be enough for you.

Whew, so I began to delve more deeply into what is enough. How much is enough? Is it, just, right? Evidently, it's just right. Is perfect, right? What is perfect? Is it just right and/or enough? When we have enough, we say this is perfect. I'm good. This is just right. Right?

So, is enough the gage for perfect? And is that what I'm striving for? Is that a set-up or is that who I already am? Not enough is part of the illusion that I am missing something. I'm not whole or complete because being enough suggests that you have all you need always. How do I know this without being a know-it-all? A know-it-all is constantly trying to prove what they know because they fear that they don't know. When you know from an inner place of knowing – faith – which is the assurance that you know you are enough, then that's all you will ever experience. Right?! That's ENOUGH! Well maybe not yet.

This inner place of knowing was forcing me to ask deeper questions regarding "being enough" for who, what and why??? This pondering brought me back around to the God of my yesteryears who I was told judged one for not being "righteous enough" to earn the love, support, and protection of Jesus.

Well, I was soon to know about love on a whole different plane as I prepared myself to get on a plane that would land me in the arms of my Osun – goddess of LOVE.

Chapter Five
~ Initiation? Really?! Yes Really! ~

Imperfectly perfect or not, it was hard for me to fathom what else could possibly be in store for me. Over the years as I immersed myself deeper into the study and practice of the multi-faceted 6000-year-old spiritual tradition called Ifa, priestess initiation continued to come through during many of my oracle divinations. The process of initiation is likened to a spiritual rebirthing and rite of passage into the next stage of spiritual self-mastery and life purpose. For me I was being called to seal the bond as an embodied priestess of the Orisa energy known as Osun. She not only called me to become her priestess – she called me to return home to Nigeria where this tradition originated for my formal initiation. I would soon find out that in returning home to the black luminous continent of Africa for my initiation, that I would begin opening the flood gates of dormant memories of many lifetimes ago – as "Keeper of the Sacred Feminine Mysteries", the "Serpent Wisdom", and the "Sacred Sexual Arts" very much associated with the "Sacred Prostitute". All of which were going to prove to be tantamount to my continued personal and spiritual growth and development.

I arrived at the compound of my Baba/Spiritual godfather and Iya/Spiritual godmother in Oyo State, Nigeria, home of the Orisa Sango, their historical King, on Christmas Eve 1994 in a flurry of anticipation and discovered that the entire state of Oyo had been in darkness for five months. On the eve of the first day of my spiritual rebirth, in the pitch blackness and stifling heat of the night, I lay in my bed desperately imagining what enormous responsibility must lie before me. Suffocating under a blanket of heat in this very hot country I was seduced into a dream like state and remember awakening moist, dizzy in a hypnotic trance just before dawn struggling into another lifetime, hearing the whispered echoes of the Ancient Mothers calling to me once again as I began to journey into the other realms...

As I slid deeper inside this ancient portal beyond space and time, I remembered my spirit from another lifetime was indelible marked at my birth and intermittent daunting images of a raging winged beast repeatedly plunging me into the belly of the abyss-darkness. Driving the raspy remnants of my innocence deeper and deeper into the carnage of my memory as I earnestly screamed for the liberation of my ancient soul. Then at age thirteen, the sacred number of mystical death and resurrection, I emerged from the darkened mist of the ancient waters and smoldering flames of the fire like the phoenix and surrendered my mind, body, and spirit in service **The Great Mother.**

I remembered walking along a very dark corridor and breathing in the echoed whispers of the Ancient Mothers of Mu chanting my name. Reeese. Reeese. Reeese, come my dear. This way. Come my dear. I deeply inhaled their sweet vibratory sounds asking me Do You Know Who You Are? My pulse quickened with a burning vibration of unbridled anticipation. I followed the chorus of their melodic voices anointing my spirit in a fragrance of delight and surrounding my body in a rainbow-colored halo of light, calling to me, from within me and around me – Do You Know Who You Are. As I exhaled, the cool rush of my spirit slithered along the narrowing spine of this ancient labyrinth deeply imbedded within the cave of my mind's eye. Volcanic eruptions of sacred geometrical shapes were vividly spewed out from the altar of my mind forming an illuminating holographic vision of my Divine purpose which I remembered was first whispered as the gentle melodic vibrations of my name... Reeese into my left ear just moments after my birth and then intricately veiled throughout my childhood rapture as I innocently and intuitively awaited the echoes of their call.

Reeese. Reeese. Reeese, come my dear. A rose-colored light pulsated in and around my feet and illuminated each of my steps as I methodically moved along the winding spiraling path that ebbed and flowed beneath my feet. Each step revealed a liturgy of ancient knowledge encrypted within the marrow of my spine, now to be impregnated in the fertile womb of my mind. Reeese. Reeese. Reeese, come my dear. The deafening rush of heat felt like a roar of silent bliss that effortlessly glided me into a voluminous repository of ancient knowing. Cool, spacious crystallized fossils of wisdom penetrated the shadows of my being and seductively aroused an innate desire that pulled and pushed the threads of my fragmented spirit, along the passageway leading down into the hush of my divine mystical cavern and up into the melodic hum vibrating within the sacred chamber of the Ancient One – ME. I remembered that lifetime initiation into… Reeese – Keeper of the Sacred Feminine Mysteries. I AM.

…As I slowly opened my eyes, rushing back through the space and time governing this lifetime, I heard the sweet sound of my Iya's voice saying wake up, come my dear, come, the mysteries of Osun await you, it's time. My room was illuminated with a golden glow and the images of the Ancient Mothers coalesced into the four sweet, dark spiritual midwives who silently stood in my room waiting to usher me into the "Osun Rebirth/Initiation" my soul had been longing for.

Over the next few years, Osun, revealed the essence of her true energy as the sacred erotic magnetic force of attraction in nature. She unveiled her universal archetypal self to me in her myriad of forms. Yes, as the ancient Khemetic goddess Het-Heru – Hathor, the Greek goddess Aphrodite, as Venus the Roman goddess, the Essene Mary Magdalene sacred sexual prostitute to (Jesus more ancient historically known as Yeshua), and the Hindu goddess Lakshmi just to name a few. These feminine goddesses and priestesses are all expressions of Lord Shiva's divine mate, Shakti, and are metaphorically associated with sacred sexuality and the energy of the planet of love –Venus. Yes! You heard me – LOVE – and in many of these ancient traditions as the "Sacred Sexual Prostitute". Here we go again... this is the highest form of LOVE and orgasmic Ascension... not primal sex, being sold for or selling oneself for sex, not using sex for enticement or addiction. NO, Sacred Sexual energy called forth to recreate "Heaven on Earth".

As I bathed in her rich sensual herstory she guided me into the cosmic arms of the Sun God Shiva, my Beloved, who manifest in the Ifa tradition as the Yoruba King Sango, Osun's Sacred Consort. Again, within the many paths as the Khemetic sky god Heru – Horus, Hindu Lord Krishna and believe it or not one more time Yeshua/Jesus known as son of God. This cosmic overview of the sacred sexual interplay of these divinities and their Divine function in the act of creation propelled me to reexamine, as one who embodies the energy of Osun, my Divine purpose in the act of creation and Divine procreation. This forced me to look at the diluted emphasize that I had placed on my earthly intimate relationships that kept failing. Once again, I began to understand more deeply that my never-ending innate desire to enter into union with my Divine beloved on the mundane plane was my desire to reconnect with "The Beloved" I re-experienced in my Perfect Sacred Union cosmic journey home. This was the longing that was driving me crazy and leaving me constantly unfulfilled.

I began to also comprehend at a soul level why my intimate relationships felt so empty and void, and in hindsight where destined to fail. As if I were watching a reel-to-reel tape, I witnessed many lifetimes of failed reunions with the "Beloved" unfold before me. Not realizing that these failed reunions where all a culmination of my aborted attempts at finding my way back home to ME. All of me! In essence I was looking for my beloved in all the wrong places. It was time to look only within me.

My Osun initiation was helping me to understand that all these different stages of my life were initiations, and initiation is not easy. This initiation helped me to grow into and gain deeper knowledge from what I had to strip away for me to step into and onto the next glorious stage of me. This was the conscious journey toward self-realization, self-mastery and ultimately my journey into my priesthood. Also, as a healer I was being called to "healer heal thyself". To reach down deep, ignite the hidden rays of light seeking to radiate my souls' journey from within the womb of darkness. All the luminous light comes forth once you cleanse and purify that which can no longer serve you within the darkness.

Chapter Six
~ Recovering from the Fall from Grace ~

Now having crossed that bridge of awareness Osun began the process of consciously reuniting me with the part of me that needed to remember my lifetime as "MaFaRaEL, Keeper of the Serpent Wisdom (kundalini) and the Sacred Sexual Arts". This lifetime remembrance was pivotal so that I could reclaim the real truth associated with my spiritual sexual legacy. My awareness and understanding of the sacred usage of my sexual energy needed to be revolutionized and evolutionized. Reviewing my lifetime as **MaFaRaEL** afforded me the opportunity to peruse the cavities from within that lifetime of perhaps any sacred sexual transgressions and subsequent violations of my most sacred vows to the "**Great Mother**", and how all these other lifetime dramas were cellularly affecting my current lifetime reality. With great remorse I prayed for this karmic juncture of my journey to soon come to an end. Once again, I ethereally traveled and remembered…

> …*The ominous sight of those enormous doors stretching high up toward the sky was now beginning to bleed through the veil of my remembrance. Time had ceased to exist, as I silently lay tormented in the wilderness of my own self-doubt and shame. How many lifetimes have I lived trapped in a hypnotic spell of powerless dominion? The remnants of my mind methodically perusing the universe for you while desperately seeking to know why you let me go… My heart aching for you, my Beloved, we've danced for so long apart. Alone. Separated. I searched. I waited. Dancing breathlessly for eons with my own not knowing. Why did you let me go? For ten thousand years, the bittersweet memory of your inevitable return still permeates my core as I stand in the shadow of our love*

beckoning toward the sun. And blinded, my King, you never see me. Continuously I lament over our time together being too short, too brief. I repeatedly hold onto the fading sounds of your voice. Whispering to me like an echo of magical tones coursing through my veins. Pumping life intravenously into an endless tube destined to produce another failed reunion.

I lay here in the wilderness of my own insanity listening to the silent thunderous sound of my heartbeat racing against time. Time to do things differently. Time to change. Time to love and forgive. Time to heal a heart filled with the remnants of ancient rage. Time to return to the timeless essence of my soul's longing. Time to complete a lifetime with you, my beloved. Time. I need time. Time to remember... I remember the deafening sound of those doors slamming shut with an intensity that still reverberates through my cellular body and the fibers of my heart with such an icy rage of finality. Shutting me out of a lifetime to grow old with you. Shutting me out of a lifetime of stolen blissful moments. Time. I need more time. Please reopen the doors, my beloved. The sound of those doors shutting me out from the completion of my own rediscovery haunts my mind like the continuous rewinding of a diabolical nightmare.

Stripped of my divine inheritance, Keeper of the Serpent Wisdom, for ten thousand years translated in the imprints of my heart as an eternity, forever, to be lost in the wilderness of my sexual longings, alone and without you. Banished, like scattered pieces of a distant memory held together by the dangling threads of unfulfilled desires. Washed over and over again in a sea of emotionally arousing preoccupations left me destined to live lifetimes distracted by the penetratingly sensuous memories of our glorious and wondrous strolls along the shores of our origin. Breathing in the intoxicating honeysuckle and jasmine breeze that delicately swirled around my thighs. Gently lifting the vibrantly golden embroidery surrounding the hem of my gown, revealing the sweet scent of autumn rain and the delicate hint of the sacred sexual *mysteries. I cherished those blissfully fatal moments. Submerging myself in the enchanting words of wisdom serenading my begging ears, with breathless exchanges beneath a moonlit sky forbidding a yielding desire to usher forth those ancient secrets, secrets too sacred to pass from my lips, I revealed no more of the sacred feminine mysteries in my fall from grace as I sealed my destiny to you. I remembered...*

Through this remembrance I was being called to transcend my fall from grace. I was starting to weave the pieces together of these different lifetimes and began to see how they were the womb imprints feeding my major core wounds of abandonment, not good enough and perfection, and how they related to the imperfect perfect longing for sacred union, again, with my beloved. As I began looking deeper into what was revealed about the perfect sacred union, I began to remember at a much deeper level this sense of abandonment and punishment as I began to fall into the unbridled sensation of duality. I felt unprotected on this earthly plane of existence and began to forget our original oneness, and that we came as a harmonious Elohim/Creator God, to co-create humanity.

However, when humanity continued destroying themselves during another "apocalyptic fall from grace", my human remembrance took that on as a sign of not being good enough to honor my calling and universal covenant once again – without you.

That forgetting of who I AM was the beginning of my fall from grace, and lifetime after lifetime my arduous journey seeking the perfect sacred reunion with the divine masculine aspect of God my co-creator. Instead, I experienced, witnessed, and only remembered the things on this earth plane that violated and dishonored the sacred feminine womb of God. I needed to know that no matter what those human devastations were, it did not define my greatness – my ONENESS with the Divine masculine.

Now this took me so deep inside the core of me as **MaFaRaEL**

– the Serpent Wisdom Keeper within that ancient Egyptian/Ethiopian pyramid. The civilization of Ethiopia was in what appeared to be an irreparable "fall from grace". Trembling and slowly falling to my knees, I began to remember all of it… during the full moon time of the month, as the **MaFaRaEL**, I was called to be in Sacred Union with my Beloved King inside the King's Chamber for what I didn't realize would be my final Sacred Sexual Ascension journey – home.

Within the Kings Chamber was where we would utilize our divine sacred sexual essence and frequency to ascend into the cosmic womb which contained the all-knowing aspect of God. From this dimension the King was able to receive the higher cosmic knowledge to bring back to humanity and maintain a just society, which the Ethiopian/Egyptian civilization desperately needed at this time. You see from…

Within my holy altar
the gentle pulsation of desire became intoxicatingly haunting.
I could feel the subtle roar of anticipation anxiously beating within my heart center.
For seven years I prepared my body temple for the next seven nights
of blissful
sacred reunion.

Three nights prior to the new moon we engaged separately in sacred cleansing and purification rituals.
Each night just before dawn we would awaken simultaneously from our sleep
and gracefully slip into the sacred chamber, which was filled with a heavy pungent mist.
Our hearts instinctively drew us together

> *with a deep longing for **sacred reunion***
> *while our bodies*
> *arched*
> *toward divine transcendence.*
>
> *The taste of sweet ambrosia from his mouth, full tender lips*
> *and tongue*
> *intuitively cleansed away the residue of ancient fear encasing*
> *my heart and belly.*
> *Caressed in his love*
> *I tenderly anointed his head and his feet,*
> *cooling the internal fires of his longing with the sacred oils of*
> *spikenard and myrrh,*
> *healing the ancient wounds embedded in his heart center and*
> *loins.*
>
> *Sanctified of our earthly carnal trappings*
> *we merged*
> *just before dawn on the seventh night, and with purified heart,*
> *mind, and body*
> *wrapped our spirit in an eternal embrace and blissfully*
> *surrendered to the Beloved in... **Sacred Reunion.***

This Sacred Union reawakened an ancient longing that I was not willing to ever let go of again. However, as **MaFaRaEL** it was my promise to initiate the chosen women of the Palace into this ancient tradition as Sacred Sexual Consorts to assist the King and his palace emissaries in transcending into the higher cosmic realms. "No! No, I will not release my Sacred Reunion with my King to another. I've waited an eternity for our reunion," I screamed, even though this is my earthly covenant.

I felt in my heart that this was not about lust and primal sexual connection. My reconnection with him in that lifetime was likened to Mary the Magdalene, who was there for Jesus, anointing and igniting him into his Christ/Christo's resurrection. Our resurrection and ascension back into our Perfect Sacred Union. "Only I am to be in the Kings Chamber. No, I will not initiate the others," I continued screaming.

And the whispered echoes of the Ancient Mothers silently screamed into my ears, "Do you know who you are?"

"No, I will not release my Sacred Reunion with my King to another," I screamed for the last time.

Their whispered echoes reverberated inside my womb, repeatedly. "**MaFaRaEL**, Keeper of the Serpent Wisdom, you are releasing your sacred sexual womb covenant to **The Great Mother**." Powerless, I surrendered my sacred throne in the underground womb of the pyramid, which was symbolic of a fetus that is unable to be birthed from the womb of darkness. And trapped and abandoned, my King never came for me. This became my fall from grace for 10,000 years.

My fall from grace was connected to me believing that I had lost him/me during the destruction of my/our Perfect Sacred Union, and Ethiopia's "fall from grace". This is what activated the rage toward this vengeful patriarchal hypocritical version of the masculine God that I was rebelling against for leaving me from the time I came out of my mother's womb.

During this dualistically destructive time for humanity, my fall from Grace was connected to me believing that our Perfect Sacred Union was being severed once again. You see, I only wanted to remember our Oneness, and I did not believe during that lifetime in Ethiopia, that we could save humanity and recreate a new world. Those original sacred feminine and divine masculine principles were on a decline and Egypt/Ethiopia was "falling from grace".

There was this need to feel safe, to feel valued, to feel enough. However, I knew no matter what this devastation had been lifetimes ago, I could no longer allow it to define my authentic greatness so that I could live in alignment with the absolute truth, which was: I Am the Perfect Sacred Union. Before I could reconnect with my Beloved Twin Flame, this inner fire, and sensual longing had to first be cleansed and purified, reconsecrated, reignited, and resurrected within me and that was The ABSOLUTE TRUTH. And, perhaps during this time, even Ethiopia shall rise again!

Queen Mother Osunnike

Part THREE
Living in Alignment with Absolute Truth

I AM

I MAKE NO APOLOGIES

I make no apologies
for who I Am.
I Am God Spirit
rooted in Her Image and spoken out of His Knowledge.
My delicate energy comes from a Supreme Being.
I Am the water
that flows from the Nile
full of barrels of gold,
diamonds, rubies, emeralds, and pearls
that first lined the pyramid walls.
I am the essence
of Divine self-taught mastery
and Divine expressions
of nature's deeply rooted gifts and treasures.
My body radiates
an ultra-fine energy
that projects Light beams
of love
causing stars
to twinkle
magnificently
in perfect universal harmony.
My tongue
lavishly
stores words of wisdom
to restore buried pictures
sacred
to my soul.
I Am the dawn
the early morning light
the Truth of the world
the darkness
that permeates the night.
I Am the sun
and the moon

*all these things
flow rhythmically through my nature.
A sparrow of thought
can last a million years.
Yet time stands still
on these bountiful hills.
Hills of nature calling
thrusting forth
and bursting
with seeds of everlasting knowledge.
I Am Who I Am
Let there be no mistake.
God's gifts are flowing.
It's an endless reservoir
And from Him
I must take
My bosom overflows
with honey and milk
from her Divine well
I drink until I Am drunk
Her Divine Essence
intoxicating my mind
and still
I remember
with penetrating stillness
who I Am
I make no apologies
I Am...*

From The Womb Of Darkness All Life Comes Forth.

Chapter Seven
~ Honoring Me First, then My Beloved Came Along ~

During this next stage of my life, I was honoring just "being with me" and started practicing Conscious Celibacy which provides an opportunity for healing and recovering from personal and intergenerational past sexual traumas.

During this process one can begin cultivating, liberating, elevating, and channeling our sensual and sexual energy. Conscious Celibacy becomes an opportunity to delve deeper in loving ourselves more unconditionally and strengthening our personal connection to the Divine. In addition, it provides an opportunity for you to learn more about what healthy relationships are, and are not, so that you can remember who you really are, and how to be partnered in an Evolutionary Relationship.

I was consciously choosing to use my energy to manifest a new life and a new way of manifesting a new life. I embraced the reclamation of my body temple and anticipated new life... once again.

This felt so good. I also delved even deeper into my spiritual tools of healthy eating, affirmative prayer, libations, meditation, yoga, breath work, and focus and concentration rituals. I began to feel absolutely certain that my unbearable cold, dreary days residing in Boston – the city of my birth – were coming to an end. With precision, I held the declaration that Jamaica (the country I had blissfully escaped to and fell madly in love with over the past ten years) shall become more than a vacation pilgrimage; it will become my permanent tropical sanctuary. Wow!

And within six month I was living in my new earthly home! Jamaica!!! Yeah, now that's what I'm talking about. Sure, enough… manifesting your dreams.

This was a major transition that could not have gone any smoother than if I had hired an angel to work out all the details. Well, when you have a guardian Orisa named Osun, really, your heart's desire is a done deal. There, in Jamacia, I was gifted with the opportunity to do my life's work at a tropical healing sanctuary right on the ocean. I had everything I dreamed of wanting. Well, everything except my true beloved.

During my time in this tropical haven, my heart, mind, and body temple greeted the four directions and elements each morning in a prayer of gratitude and thanksgiving for this subsequent return to one of the planetary wombs of **The Great Mother** that I felt such a strong connection with. Amidst this tropical panacea, where my mind and spirit slid into the rhythm of nature, I listened intently to the whispered echoes of the Ancient Mothers every day.

And I began speaking that vibrational language far more often. The first time it came through me, I was visiting one of the amazing caves. As soon as I walked in, there was a very familiar, ancient, and new feeling flowing through me. I remember bats would begin to swoop down and fly past my ears almost every time I visited that cave, and I would hear them say, "Listen… Do you know who you are."

This cave and Jamaica were hauntingly and beautifully familiar. What on earth was it about me and Jamaica?

And then one day, at the crack of dawn while doing some yoga postures, I had a major spontaneous remembrance. I began to see a very old ship coming up toward the reef, and it was filled with so many enslaved ancestors brought in from Ghana. As I continued journeying back in time, yes, I was one of them. I saw myself in shackles and felt the pain between my legs from the horrific rapes that I had experienced on that ship during that arduous journey. How could anyone do this to a woman? To me – a woman who had been a Queen Mother in another lifetime that felt like it had been eons ago. I was remembering my journey, my first journey into Jamaica during that lifetime. During the most demanding time, somehow I was able to not only survive, but to also thrive after escaping deep into the cavernous caves and higher up into the mountainous regions with the empowered revolutionary Maroon women.

Yes, I was remembering and doing my very best to listen to the Ancient Mothers. But no matter how much I listened to their whispers, roaring like the sea, I couldn't comprehend what my own body temple was trying to convey.

I could still sense the remnants of this Beloved. "Who are you?" I would silently scream.

I felt him close in the ethers of my mind, as if he were my breath. So close. There was a part of me that found it hard to fully embrace what felt like was his inevitable return. Yet, another worldly apprehension would fill my belly with a hypervigilance of what I didn't know. Whenever I would reminisce over previous failed relationships, my heart would retreat into an empty darkness that heralded a lifetime perhaps meant to be lived alone.

Eventually, the hunger for his love abated, and I quenched my intermittent thirst for "sacred union" with gratitude that he would surface when, where, and how he was to surface. Besides, I was in the bosom of a tropical sensual erotic menagerie of masculine energy that engaged and embraced my occasional desire for male companionship – nothing more.

However, about six months later, there inside the loving congenial womb of "Mother Nature" my womb rebelled for the second time. Depleting all I had; my womb began expelling thick red angry clots of blood from my now exhausted body for no less than 11 to 13 days within a lunar cycle. How could this be? I was in heaven, doing healing work that I loved in the bosom of nature. I listened effortlessly to the soothing sound of waves from the ocean, literally a few feet away, creating a natural healing symphony for everyone… except me.

How could my body temple betray me in this way? I was listening:

> *Watch your belly, watch your head, come round sundown cool your body and be still… listen. Relax, surrender, and follow your Truth follow your Truth follow your Truth…*

These were some of the whispered echoes heard from the Ancient Mothers that I listened to and honored daily.

But what Truth was I not following??? This was unbelievable and unacceptable. After almost a year of such mixed messages, my body temple, weak and confused, surrendered in a serendipitous way – relieved – to undergo yet another surgical violation to my womb… the fibroid tumors were back.

I returned to Boston's gray skies, howling wind, piles and piles of snow, and homelessness. The surgical mutilation was a success, and this time my doctor skillfully removed 36 fibroid tumors – twice as many as before – while leaving my traumatized uterus still intact. What the hell were these womb violating predators trying to do to me, or perhaps tell me? Desperately missing and longing for my Jamaican abode, I bowed in gratitude and turned my focus to my recovery and more practical matters – securing a bedroom in my sister's house.

In gratitude, looking through a spiritual lens I realized I could take this much needed space and time to spiritually ponder, Now What The Hell Is All Of This About? And I did. I also allowed the thoughts of my beloved to fade into the background of my life. My heart and womb were deep in lockdown – I mean recovery – for at least six weeks. And did I mention I was homeless?

My loving and caring sister opened her home, which gave us time to reminisce on those holier days gone by, present circumstances, and future desires. And regarding future desires, I began to envision that when I returned to Jamaica I would have my own "Sacred Healing Nest" retreat center to support women in the healing of their wombs… and that was going to require official documents. I applied, and if you know anything about the Caribbean, you know everything is about hurry up and wait. The concept of time in the tropics is attuned to Saturn's clock and calendar. I waited and waited for my official work permit from the Jamaican government, which would allow me the southern comfort of returning home with a PERMENANT work visa, which, of course, never came.

In the meantime, six months or more back in the belly of the beast – America – I resumed the life I had fled. While waiting to return to my ideal Jamaican life, I reestablished my healing practice, which now extended into New York and Washington DC. And while I was providing some amazing healing work for others, another echoed message from the Ancient Mothers came loud, louder, and even louder…

You will be married by December… listen.

Oh, I was listening and watching and laughing my butt off. "OK mothers, December is just six months away. That's going to take a lot of magic. You're kidding right? Six months…"

While waiting for that Jamaican work permit, and to take my mind off this six-month miracle brewing in the ethers, I began thinking about other places here in the Americas that I might want to pitch a tent. Or perhaps, if a place somewhere in the USA seduced my spirit like the seductive energy of Jamaica, I might be enticed to purchase land and build the "Sacred Nest" healing center for myself and others with a similar calling.

Over the next few months, I really enjoyed my work traveling back-and-forth to New York and DC, meeting new people, and doing some phenomenal healing work. Yeah, this was great. And then, strangely enough, one of the colleagues that I was working with developed a website for me and a few other healers, highlighting the different types of spiritual practices that each of us were providing. My page was definitely a reflection of the many paths I had been journeying along over the years. From yoga, breathwork, transpersonal therapy, theatre arts, and yes, of course, now a priestess of Osun.

Well, the next thing I know, I received an email from an Ifa Priest named Baba Koleoso who shared how much he liked the website and the diversity of the different Priests and our specialties. When I reached out to thank him, I found out that I was the only one who responded. Wow, and I was so happy that I did. This brother seemed like a reflection of me – different, curious, passionate... and did I say different?! The higher wisdom, intuitive knowledge, his soft no-nonsense vocal intonation was refreshing and anointing. After several conversations which really highlighted our similarities, I began to wonder if he might be the husband that I was told would be coming. *Oh, I'm listening Mothers...*

You see, there was something familiar about him. So, as I was getting ready for our next conversation, I decided that I was going to speak with him about this familiar feeling. I began our conversation with, "So Baba, how have you been, since we last spoke about the power of spirit, the Orisa, and how it works in our lives?"

He said, "Wow, thank you for asking because it's been challenging and from what I'm beginning to feel from you, I know you would understand me."

"Of course, Baba. What's happening?" I asked.

He went on to share with me the struggles he was experiencing as a Priest, who knows about the universal power that brought him back from his own two near death experiences. He said, "I know how this power works, but I'm trying to help my wife heal from multiple sclerosis and something's not working."

Well, four months into the six, what on earth did I hear him say *WIFE*? No, obviously, he was not the husband I was going to be married to in December. So, I thought…

And, then he said, "Sister, as a Priestess and healer, would you please give some thought to what I maybe missing? I remember reading on your website some of the healing work that you provide. I mean, you do energy healing work and guide clients into other lifetimes and the trauma that they're holding onto in this lifetime, is that right?"

"I'm open to whatever may come through you regarding my wife. Thank you and I look forward to talking with you soon."

"Absolutely, Baba." OK, so now I was much clearer about what this meeting was really about. So, I thought...

Following up on his request, I did tap in, and some amazing things came through about his wife. The next time we spoke, I asked to be able to share what had come through with her directly. Oh, my goodness, what I shared resonated with her and the next thing I know, I was being invited by them both to come to Kentucky for a week to do some deeper work for her. Wow, Kentucky! What part of the planet is Kentucky on? Well, I would soon find out.

Chapter Eight
~ Not Kentucky Fried Chicken ~

Seeing Baba for the first time at the airport was simultaneously familiar and strange. Baba said he wanted to make sure I had something good to eat, and that I got an interesting taste of Kentucky.

Relaxing into his energy, I smiled and said jokingly, "That sounds great, as long as it's not Kentucky Fried Chicken."

"No worries.", he said. "Kentucky is a lot more than that chicken. Trust me."

I did trust him.

He took me to what had been an old plantation that had been restored as a cultural center and restaurant called the Java House, by a friend of his, an African American woman. After eating dinner, Baba asked her if she would show me more of this old new space.

As I walked through this structure, I could feel the pain, suffering and hardship imposed upon human beings due to a blatant disregard for the divine principles of life and a dishonoring of the Sacred Feminine. I knew the suffering had been endured, not only by so many enslaved ancestors, but also had silently enveloped the white women, who thought they ruled that plantation, perhaps, oblivious to their own sexual oppression.

When Baba's friend took me out onto the land in the backyard, I had to stop in front of this very large tree and kneel. She acknowledged that I was tapping into all the women and men whose souls were still energetically trapped, when their bodies were hung from those branches.

After what seemed forever, Baba lifted me from the ground, and we went back inside. As we went upstairs, to my surprise, I began to see where one of the performance rooms had been a ballroom, like you see in the movies, with white people dancing in old costume clothing and black people dressed as servants serving refreshments. This was like something out of a movie. But in that moment, it was familiar and for real for me. I told them both what was coming through. She thanked me for sharing, and said that Baba had been helping her to spiritually cleanse the place, because years later some parts of it still held the energy of the plantation. Baba shared that with all the work that was being done, the energy of many of the ancestors were still struggling to move on.

That's what I felt when she took me up into the attic to show me some of the different artifacts that had been found on the property. I began to feel cold, angry, and creepy, as I looked at this long box that looked like a wooden coffin. With my hand shaking and tears in my eyes, I pointed to it and asked her, "What is that?"

I felt Baba place his hand on my back, as she said, "Oh, you don't know about that. It's a breeding box. The slave masters would select some of the really strong men and very fertile women on the plantation, lock them inside the box and force them to breed."

"How the hell could they do that?" I hissed.

"If they resisted, they and/or their family members were tortured or killed; that's how the hell that was done.", he said.

I had studied a lot about slavery, but I had never heard of breeding boxes. This was horrifying and my mind was trying to take me there or show me something. "I need to use the bathroom," I said, needing to get the hell out of that dungeon.

On the one-hour drive to his house in Lexington, he shared with me that Kentucky is "Horse Country" and some of the best breed horses on the planet are here in Kentucky.

"Here, in Kentucky, some of the breeding that they do to make these phenomenal racehorses may be natural, and some of it not at all. However, that's the same mentality that was used for breeding humans – to create those slave breeding boxes. I know this is a lot and you must be tired," he said.

Oh, I was dead tired. That was the beginning of my first night in Kentucky. Maybe, I just should have asked to go to KFC instead.

During the drive, and feeling into this Kentucky energy, I started asking myself, "What is this trip really about?"

As if reading my mind, Baba suggested I close my eyes and rest, and I did. This was strange for me because the only man I ever felt comfortable enough with to close my eyes and drift into sleep, while in the car, was my daddy when he would drive us on long trips at night. Other than that, the only driver I trusted, especially at night, was me. I began to awaken just as he was pulling into his driveway. Baba wasn't sure whether his wife was still up or not. Either way, he was going to take me and my things to the bedroom so that I could get some real rest.

As we walked inside his house, we heard water running in the kitchen sink. "Sounds like she's still up," he said. The house felt warm, cozy, and holy; yes, you heard me… holy. "It's a good thing you had a little nap because she probably wants to talk to you just a little bit before we all turn in," he said with a smile on his face. As we walked into the kitchen, he called out her name, "Rashida, Osunnike is here. Remember, she's here to do the healing work with you this week."

"Of course, I remember!" she blurted out. "Hey sister, come on in, come on in."

As I walked over to the sink to greet her, we paused and looked into each other's eyes, as if we had always known one another. There was an odd kind of familiarity there.

Over the next few days, we did some very deep and powerful energy healing and past life regression work. She delved deeper than I could have imagined. And our oddly familiar connection grew deeper. It seemed like she felt that she could trust me in reference to some of her personal challenges. After three days of some very wonderful healing work, we began to conclude the formal work and just hang out and get to know each other a little better.

And, in the midst of this fun, she began looking deep into my eyes and spoke into my heart a very deep and profound question, "Osunnike," she said slowly and deliberately, "Can I ask you a question?"

"OK," I said.

"Thank you for coming and doing all of this so called healing with me."

"No problem," I said. "It's truly an honor."

And, then she interrupted me and said, "I'm wondering if you would join our family?"

What did she just say? I said to myself! I guess she saw the confused look on my face, laughed, and asked me the question again. She saw that I was still in a daze, so she called out to Baba with an urgency saying, "Come here! Come here! come here!"

He hurried into the kitchen and said, "What's wrong? Is everything OK?"

With a big smile on her face, she said, "Yes, I just asked Osunnike if she would join our family."

Baba looked at me, then looked at her, and then they both looked at me... her with a smile on her face, and him with a smile that was silently saying, "Am I hearing what I'm hearing?"

Oh, as they both looked at me, I was still in a daze and to my surprise, I heard myself say, "Ah, yes."

What did I just say?

We hugged each other, then Baba said, "Let's get some really good food and celebrate." And while Rashida was telling him what she was hungry for, I began trying to digest what this *really* means and *who is this man... really*?

To my surprise, there were more celebratory events to come. At the close of the first week, I got to partake in my first Native American sweat lodge ceremony. I had been longing to take part in a sacred sweat lodge ceremony for many years in Boston. Now, here I was in Kentucky with my soon-to-be husband, who just so happened to not only be an Ifa high priest, but also a Inipi/sweat lodge water pourer, within the Native American Lakota tradition. What I didn't know at that time was that the sweat lodge was also symbolic of the earth womb. Baba held these ceremonies monthly in Lexington at the Adena mound, which was a sacred Indigenous Ancestral ceremonial mound.

That night I could feel the energy on the mound, so strong, vibrating all around me. This whole environment was amazing, and it was 60° in December, really different from December in Boston. I began to think, wow, I could do 60° in December in Kentucky... we'll see.

I couldn't take my eyes off Baba, as I watched him doing all these sacred rituals to begin this amazing cleansing and purifying ceremony. I also began noticing that there was something very familiar about it; yet, I was thinking to myself, *How would I know this?* However, there were parts of me that knew, and I felt the sacred vibrations under my feet. Yup, this was just the beginning.

As I entered the lodge, I was seated next to Rashida, who was seated next to Baba at the opening of the lodge. After the heated rocks had all been set in place, and began to dimly light up the lodge, I could see the faces of those who had joined us. I could also feel their spirits and yet, I had no clue of what was going on.

While we were still in the first of four rounds of the ceremony and prayers being uplifted by Baba, I began to sense someone who felt ancient, sitting on the right side of me. Looking through my peripheral vision, I could see a woman who appeared to be very old, with two long white braids. My first thoughts were, *I don't remember seeing this woman on the land standing with us before the ceremony began inside the lodge. Maybe she slipped in later? When did she arrive, and when did she come into the lodge? I mean, am I really seeing what I'm seeing out of the corner of my eye?*

Then, it was like she was listening to my thoughts, and she quickly turned her head to look at me and, as our eyes met, she said, "I am Maathra, medicine woman! Then we both went back to looking into the luminescent light coming from the rocks.

Quietly startled, I began looking at the other people in the lodge to see if they were seeing and hearing who just spoke out loud to me. Everyone seemed like they were in their own world and not distracted by Maathra. By the time we got to the final round, I was soaking wet, and in another world while staring once again into the light shimmering from the rocks. At the end of the ceremony, when we came out of the lodge, the darkness was illuminated by the full moon. I searched and searched but did not see Maathra.

At the end of the night, once we were back at the house, I shared with Baba what I experienced and asked him, if he saw Maathra there in the sweat lodge. He said, "No, Osunnike, I didn't see this woman. She showed herself to you for you. Everyone has their own experiences in the sweat lodge. I'm sure she will make herself known to you over time."

Yes, I Joined the Family

Before leaving Kentucky, the three of us agreed that we would take some time to process what our new commitment and family configuration really meant, and what it would look like moving forward. Rashida and I hugged each other knowing that this was the beginning of a whole new life for all of us.

Yes, I knew he would come, my *Twin Flame*. I just didn't know he would come the way he came. And I certainly didn't know he would unearth my strategically buried core wounds. I didn't know that my time with him – this time – would be the catalyst to catapult me smack dab back to the passage into the womb of **The Great Mother**.

To my surprise as we were preparing to hit the road, I heard the whispered echoes of the Ancient Mother's silently speak and say loud and clear, *"Wash and anoint his feet."*

"You want me to do what?" I silently responded. Yes, I heard it again and then again.

As I explained to him about this ritual that I was being guided to do for him before we left, he said, "I really need this," and bowed his head in gratitude.

During the ritual, I was having flashbacks of my mother when she would wash and anoint my fathers' feet. Back then, I thought it was disgusting. I remember my mom telling my sister and me that, "You must always treat your husband as a King... and he needs to know that you are a Queen." I didn't share any of that with Baba.

During the ride to the airport, I was in absolute amazement that the marriage Osun predicted would happen in December was happening! Baba suggested that we stop and get something to eat and ground myself before my flight back to Boston. However, as he pulled into the restaurant parking lot, I had this overwhelming sense of anxiety and I begin crying uncontrollably. He held my hand and said, "Osunnike, please tell me what you're feeling? It's ok; I'm here, I'm feeling you and I'm listening."

And, the next thing I knew, I began remembering the ancient fateful lifetime with him, my twin flame, the King I was called to assist as his Sacred Sexual Consort, guiding his journey into the higher wisdom realms. That was the lifetime of my fall from grace because I failed to honor my covenant, as **MaFaRaEL** and was banished from the temple and he did not save me. I began sharing with him…

> …*My heart is still aching for you, my Beloved. We've danced for so long apart. Alone. Separated. I searched. I waited. Dancing breathlessly for eons with my own not knowing. Why did you let me go? For ten thousand years, the bittersweet memory of your inevitable return still permeates my core as I stand in the shadow of our love beckoning toward the sun. And blinded, my King, you never see me. Continuously I lament over our time together being too short, too brief. I repeatedly hold onto the fading sounds of your voice. Whispering to me like an echo of magical tones coursing through my veins, pumping life intravenously into an endless destiny to produce another failed reunion after you say to me, "I am here for you".*

I cried and cried and cried. And when I stopped to catch my breath, I looked up and there were tears in Baba's eyes… as he continued that memory from an authentic knowing and true remembrance. With tears in his eyes, he looked at me and said, "I will not let anyone, or anything take you away from me again as we co-create a new world."

That was the new beginning, this lifetime, of our perfect sacred union. Over the next few months, I returned to Kentucky as we began to explore more deeply what being a polygamist family would be like for us. Baba also came to Boston to meet my family, and formally stated his intentions to my sons to join in sacred union with their mother. Before he met with my mother, instead of me telling her that he was a high priest, I told her that his spiritual calling was likened to being a Bishop, and I kept the piece about it being a polygamist family to myself. She was so excited and welcomed Baba with open arms – she always wanted me to marry a Bishop. My community was also extremely supportive and told me they knew I always colored outside the lines. "Wow, this is way outside the lines, and it looks like you all are about to weave together a beautiful tapestry."

By June of that year, I had moved to Kentucky and the perfect imperfect sacred union had begun again.

I'm Going to Live Where??? Yes, Kentucky – Just the Beginning

When I first moved to Kentucky from Boston, an African American ancestral dumping ground, I wasn't sure how I could be of service to those in this state and city of Lexington. However, as an African American, Native American, revolutionary evolutionary, healer and artist, who grew up the daughter of parents, who were not only a Pentecostal preacher and missionary back in the 50s, 60s, and 70s, they were also revolutionary evolutionaries who committed their time, energy, and money into the Freedom Riders movement to help oppressed, supposedly freed, southern black folks come to Boston and start a new life chapter. I grew up understanding their mission as *our mission* and I have carried this forward in my work with women, as *my mission*, to this day.

Now, here in the land of the Bluegrass, I was hypnotized and captivated by the strong ancestral energetic pulse that ran through the veins of the historic lands of Kentucy. Being with my Beloved Baba was very helpful in getting me acclimated, given that he was already very much aware of the history associated with Kentucky and was providing Ancestral honoring and healing. However, it was also a bit intimidating. He was not only doing his professional college administrative diversity work, he was also doing amazing healing work with men around the country.

I had to let Baba know that this transition was somewhat intimidating for me. I remember him saying "Osunnike, what are you talking about? We are here to do this work together. I've been telling the women that I have worked with over the years, that they need a Priestess with your knowledge and skillset to guide them on the next level of their spiritual journeys. That's not my work with them. I am here to uplift these men and restore our divine origins, and to inspire young men and boys to know they're here for a higher purpose. The women need that from you. Let's do this sacred feminine and divine masculine work together."

I began to study more about Kentucky's history in reference to the atrocities connected to the original Native American land caretakers, the enslaved Africans, African Americans, and White people, who were committed to their freedom and honoring the land.

Initially, it appeared to me to be a land of cultural contradictions, but with an earnest striving by some to unite. Through my work as a healer and spiritual midwife, I have had many opportunities working with Kentucky's diverse population of women spanning across the elite terrain of Kentucky's bluebloods to those impoverished in cities throughout Lexington and Louisville and the hills of Appalachia. As a result, I have come to recognize that there are some sturdy threads of commonality that run through this diverse land.

The more I began to walk the land here, the more I began to hear the voices of our ancient wise Native American, African, and European ancestors, whose blood became the sacred fertilizer to enrich this plush Kentucky land. These voices needed to speak to our hearts and remind us that we are the custodial keepers of this sacred earth. The message was clear that we may come from many diverse paths but buried deep within our hearts, wombs and spirits is one truth.

You see, for those of us within the West African spiritual tradition of Ifa, in which I had been initiated as a priestess, the reverence, communication and honoring of our ancestors is an integral ingredient for individual, family and community spiritual development, evolution, and global transformation.

The remembrance and honoring of that ancestral wisdom begins with our women. As women, we hold that ancestral cellular memory within our wombs because we are not only the original vessels who give birth to humanity, we are also the shapers of humanity. In order for women to tap into this rich ancestral wisdom and guidance, we must first come together to heal and restore our wombs. Then by nourishing, honoring, and celebrating the cultural strengths inherent within our diverse roots, we begin to renew our commitment to healing our diverse communities and planet. Thus, contributing to the healing of the womb of our *Earth Mother* and our collective human family all over the world. Remember, I emphatically believe that as "CEEWs" (Consciously Evolving Empowered Women) – we are being called to give birth to a "New World" and that we have the "Innate Power" to do so. It is our inherent feminine birthright, deeply embedded within our wombs. Now, imagine joining in healthy union with conscious evolving men, as a part of co-creating this new world mission. That's what time it is.

Wow! I began to see and feel that, perhaps, I was here to help in homogenizing this process to weave together those diverse threads into a rich mosaic – a tapestry.

With that mosaic in mind, over the next few years my work as a priestess of Osun, seeress, healer, and spiritual midwife for many women was tremendously rewarding and continued to reveal much. The presence of the Ancient Mothers had begun possessing my body temple and speaking through my mouth in foreign tongues much more frequently, while administering profound healings. During my spiritual work, my mind was constantly being bombarded with fleeting images of ritualistic cleansings, purifications, and womb healing ceremonies that I was being called to provide. There were more and more women in need of receiving these womb healings.

I also continued to see glimpses of the face of Maathra, medicine woman, from the sweat lodge ceremony. Often, she would say, *"Do you know who you are?"* This was intense, and yes, I thought I knew who I was becoming.

I also began sensing that I was being called into what felt like another initiation – an intense shamanic spiritual unfolding. I was being propelled out from where I thought I was as a spiritual midwife and into an even deeper knowing of my own womb.

Once again, those venomous fibroid tumors were attacking my womb, and my spirit was pushing and pulling me into a state of fragmented confusion.

I literally began screaming, "What is this about?! What am I missing?!" Here I was an Osun priestess and energy healer, and yet, I was becoming filled with doubts about *myself* from A to Z. I felt like an empty shell totally disconnected from who I believed I was. Frightened and helplessly numb, I desperately searched in agony for the spiritual answers to the same questions that I began consciously asking over twenty-five years ago, *"Who Am I?"* and *"Am I really good enough?"*

The very things I valued felt like they were being shattered, leaving me to stare blindly into the cosmic mirror of my own big brown eyes, which reflected the scattered fragmented images of my soul - AGAIN. This signaled the ancient rumbling of new life, which stirred within the sacred chamber of what I was now believing was an empty womb. I prayed to be delivered from whatever this ancient calling was with grace and ease this time because my Empty Womb was exhausted…

After several months of holistic healing medicine that was not working, once again, I painfully agreed to another invasive surgery to remove these reoccurring tumors from my own womb. As I opened my eyes after the procedure, Baba was holding my hand and apologetically shaking his head and whispering that this Kentucky doctor had removed the tumors and my sacred womb.

"My womb; she took my womb?!" I blurted out.

In that moment, everything I had come to know about who I Am as a womb healing spiritual midwife was being unraveled, thread by thread, as I screamed to Baba, "How can I continue contributing to changing this world and helping women heal their wombs when I couldn't even save my own…"

This question laid heavily in my spirit and on my heart once I returned home. In a curious, sad, and exhausted state, I went to my Ancestral Altar to honor them and apologize to the Ancient Mothers for what felt like dropping the baton.

As I enter the sanctuary, it's dark and hazy. The incandescent light of one candle flickers in anticipation of my priestly ritual. There is a pungent air of smoke swirling about the room. I kneel at my ancestral altar, and with a heavy heart and labored breath, I begin to pour libations, praying to my ancestors both far and near.

My spirit is weighted down under the sacred flowing white robe, I always select for this nightly communion, that adorns my body temple but is unable to lift my spirit.

Me: Omi tutu, Ile tutu, Oni tutu, tutu Orisa, tutu Egun; I pour these libations to you my Nana, Ibe se (e by a). I pour… I can't do this anymore. I don't even know if you're listening. Or if anybody really cares about what I'm dealing with.

Ancient Mothers: *Yes, my dear. They care, and WE are listening. Have you forgotten? Your altar is the sacred womb portal that you can receive divine guidance and strength from.*

Me: *I'm overwhelmed. I can't do all this anymore. It's too much.*

Ancient Mothers: *When you're looking through Robin's eyes, which only see not being "enough", then YES, it's too much.*

Me: *Enough in this case is enough. Because all I see around the world is violence, disease, and pain. I can't look at this anymore. Enough is enough.*

Ancient Mothers: *We are well aware of this human condition that has left a trail of broken hearts and wombs all around the world.*

Me: *You know what's so unbelievable, from Mama Africa, where the feminine was revered and sacred, to America and everywhere in between, sacred wombs are becoming nothing more than waste dumps.*

Ancient Mothers: *Yes, so many wombs are overflowing with rage and fear, which nourishes the destruction of your most precious commodity, the womb of the Earth Mother, and the wombs of Her daughters.*

Me: *I don't understand anymore. How did this happen? We've become the walking dead.*

Ancient Mothers: *Yes, and this is the time for humanity to reawaken. To remember being birthed from* **The Great Mother's** *womb that unites all.*

Me: *Yeah, well, too many of us are still asleep at this time. I can't do this New Age stuff anymore.*

Ancient Mothers: *The old age thrived on greed and bred insecurity. Don't you remember...*

Me: *No!!! Because I'm still boiling over with rage. I can't stand* *seeing what's happening to our sisters, and our brothers – our world – from this place of powerlessness, anymore.*

Ancient Mothers: *You have more power than you realize.*

Me: *That's madness. Mothers, please hear me... I can't help them... I can't do this! I can't do this!! I can't...*

Ancient Mothers: *You can't afford not to. One sister's womb is another sister's womb. The desecration of your wombs is a reflection of the desecration of the Earth Mother's womb. And all of humanity is responsible for care of Her Womb – one sister's womb at a time.*

Me: *Mothers, one sister's womb at a time. That will take forever.*

Ancient Mothers: *There will be No forever if you don't begin Now! This healing is vital for humanity. If the Earth Mother's womb is polluted, the womb which provides the primary nutrients for your daily existence, then how can those in this realm bring anything healthy into being... never mind... Divine.*

Me: *That's why I'm saying... our wombs have been desecrated and it's too much.... for me.*

Ancient Mothers: *Listen... This is your covenant... this is what you are here to bring forth.*

Me: *Then I've failed. I've failed* **The Great Mother** *again. I mean I couldn't even save my own womb. I just want to write, sing, dance and clap my hands to a different drum.*

Ancient Mothers: *Listen to that "Ancient Drum" and remember... who you are. YOU have forgotten who YOU are. And who's you are.*

Me: *I'll tell you what I remember... I'm a descendant of African slaves and, displaced Cherokee Indians and from what I see I have NO power to change anything.*

Ancient Mothers: *From Robin's limited lens, yes, you are powerless. But your true self, Osunnike, remembers that the way to help humanity is to first liberate your spirit. And then your spirit* *illuminates your divinity. Osunnike... remember... your divinity teaches you how to live in this world and not be a slave to the things of this world. Remember your divinity Osunnike...*

Me: Yes, yes, I need to remember my divinity. This is harder than before.

Ancient Mothers: *Your divinity enables you to honor the mystery of your womb, which imbues you with the power to create some...thing... from no... thing.*

Me: Yes mothers. Help me. Please help me to remember. I got lost...

Ancient Mothers: *You must return to the sacred altar of "Self". Return and re-collect your sacred tools so that you may strengthen your Asé... your life force.*

Me: Yes, yes. Where... where do I go...? I got lost.

Ancient Mothers: *To the "Sacred Water"; cleanse away the cobwebs of illusion so that you can bathe in the reflection of your divine light. Will you go?*

Me: Yes... yes mothers I'll go. I'll go to the water.

Translucent... gentle... intermittent... rhythmically floating encased within the depths of my womb... I remember.

Ancient Mothers: *Rise and allow the water to liberate your soul from the painful memories held within the collective intergenerational memory.*

Me: Oh, mother of my soul, I come to you empty seeking to replenish my spirit and rejuvenate my body.

Ancient Mothers: *Now Osunnike...we must journey deep into the "Sacred Earth". Feel her pulse vibrating within you. Feel the realignment of your energy centers. Can you feel her rhythm under your feet?*

Me: Yes, Oh my goddess. I feel her roar... I feel the earth alive under my feet.

Here... I... Am

solid, grounded, and rooted

in... authentic Truth... I remember.

Ancient Mothers: *Now dance... dance the dance of freedom... feel the rainbow serpent rising up your spine strengthening you from your root to your crown.*

Me: *I remember. I remember. We are the keepers of the serpent wisdom... I remember.*

Ancient Mothers: *Come... we must go to the "Sacred Fire" and burn away all doubt and transform your fears... listen.*

Me: *Yes, I remember. The flame is burning in my heart... I can see the light.*

I am the dancing blaze

igniting passion into action

I am a catalyst for transformation and illumination... Oh my God I remember.

Ancient Mothers: *Yes Osunnike. Now take in the breath... breathe... breathe in the "Sacred Air". Let each breath fill your mind, body, and spirit with unconditional love. Listen... listen.*

Me: *Oh,* **Great Mother***, as I inhale the truth of who I AM... I thank you.*

I am the dark stillness behind daylight... I remember.

Ancient Mothers: *Now go. Shine the light of unity and be the bridge between spirit and matter.*

Me: *Yes, the bridge...*

Ancient Mothers: *Remember, you are called to give birth to an initiation for women that your ancient soul set in motion long... long ago. Listen... Reeeeessse... Keeper of the Sacred Feminine Mysteries...*

Me: I remember... I remember... Oh beloved **Great Mother**... *Ancient Mothers I remember. I will honor my sacred covenant to you* **Great Mother** *and uphold the tradition of my ancient ancestors going all the way back to the stars so that I may be an enlightened bridge for all of humanity. I remember...*

Ancient Mothers: *Osunnike, this wisdom must not be lost... and your spirit cannot be broken... you are reawakening to your true power... reawakening to your inner knowing... Remember, recognize, and honor all the collective ancestral wombs stretching back seven generations and beyond. You are called to reawaken the Serpent Wisdom dormant within their wombs... listen and usher forth the...*

Me: ... Sacred Feminine Mysteries Initiation – Passage into **The Great Mother**... *I remember.*

I remembered.

Suddenly, I found myself seated back at my altar swaying from side to side like a swirling hush of energy. Wow! Here I go again, I thought. These Ancient Mothers were speaking through me, into me, from me... and I was not fully understanding how this was happening, because I didn't even remember how I remembered or did any of that communication. What exactly was I remembering? I had no clue; and I didn't even know how I knew all of this nor the depth of who I had just been communing with again.

However, I felt the embodied essence of these elemental forces within me. After what seemed to be decades, but perhaps was only a few months, I began to experience somewhere deep inside a strange sense of being brand-spanking new, and ancient at the same time. It was a very familiar, un-grounding, yet solid feeling that I somehow remembered having experienced during many of my other lifetimes. I knew I was on the threshold of another major spiritual rebirth – initiation. My "Womb" was not empty.

It Gets Even Better

Oh, my goddess! Baba and I were being called to go on a sacred pilgrimage to Peru. We felt like this trip was divinely guided and it effortlessly fell from the heavens into our arms. We began planning this as a sacred journey for ourselves and then envisioned guiding others on their sacred journeys in the future. Over the years, I had several spontaneous flashbacks from a lifetime in Peru. However, they were in bits and pieces. Baba also felt his own very strong connection to Peru, and we were gleefully curious about what was to unfold for us both. And this would be our first journey together out of the country.

On the long and arduous ride to the hotel, I was feeling a lot of chaotic energy bubbling up inside of me. Over the next couple of days, I found it difficult to partake in the first few ceremonies. Baba kept encouraging me to join in these sacred rituals, and I tried.

However, after a few days had passed, I began sensing my spirit somehow detaching from my body. Then it all began to come back together on the night before going to Machu Picchu, the highly advanced pre-Incan civilization. That night was one of the most significant nights of my life. It was the turning point for me, and the beginning of total blissful surrender.

But that day started out with me having intense emotions of anger and jealousy. And yes, those "not good enough" thoughts were resurfacing. Unfortunately, I was directing them towards Baba, but I could feel these emotions were beyond our present life connection. No, this was old, unresolved anger toward the – masculine energy. This was the ancient RAGE again!

Panic stricken, I began to realize that what I was taking out on Baba was ancient unresolved stories that needed to be cleansed and purified, once again, through the elemental altars of my soul. After a tumultuous night of anger that I had spewed all over him in the restaurant at the dinner table, in front of the group that we were traveling with, and the Peruvian shamans, I returned to our hotel room filled with a confusing mixture of deep heartfelt humiliation, unrelenting anger, and soul-filled redemption.

When Baba returned to our room, I begged him for forgiveness. He silently refused to respond to my tearful pleading. The emotional pain was so intense for both of us. Not wanting to continue trying to force my repentance upon him, I grabbed my pillow, exiled myself to the tiny bathroom, climbed into the tub and begged the Ancient Mothers for deep sleep. I just needed to get out of the painful, rage-filled torment that I was feeling and sensing in the pit of my belly. As I continued begging for sleep, I could sense within my core that the remnants of another emerging past lifetime were coming through.

That night...

> *I began experiencing myself being drawn into what felt like an eternal abyss/portal. From within this portal, I was hovering over what appeared like a vast never-ending ocean. In the next moment I was turned upside down, inside out and gently plunged head down into what seemed like a journey into the depths of the sea water. In that moment I was terrified because my physical body did not know how to swim, and I was being pulled gently and firmly into the deepest darkest depths of the ocean.*
>
> *To my amazement as I landed on what appeared to be the bottom of the ocean this bottom opened and once again, I began descending now into what appeared like an unexploded*

volcano with magnificent wild flames everywhere. I began experiencing myself as a mixture of the flames and then within the blink of an eye I was pushed back up out of the volcanic roaring flames into the floor of the ocean. It was exhilaratingly powerful to then experience being ushered up out of the ocean.

As my ever-rising gliding momentum continued lifting me higher, I witnessed an ancient aspect of myself, which appeared to be part human, reptilian, extraterrestrial and multidimensional and with its enormous dark wings, it swooped down and drew me into it, high upon an Andean mountaintop. As I landed on the mountaintop, I experienced myself as the transformation of being and witnessing ALL my beingness simultaneously. I experienced all these different aspects of myself merge and my whole body vibrated with the intensity and speed of sacred union as I traveled at the frequency of sound and light through the agonizing screams of the underworld "unattached".

The next thing I knew Baba was waking me up and saying it's time for us to get ready to go to Machu Picchu. As I began to prepare for this sacred journey I realized, like ten thousand years before, I was being gifted with the opportunity to embrace the shadows of my soul. At the same time, the light of mercy slowly pierced through the veils of my illusions, antiquated conditionings, and self-defeating limitations that desperately were clinging to my flesh.

As we ventured up into the amazing ancient empire of Machu Picchu, I knew that I had returned home from lifetimes ago. I also could see and feel the energy shifting for Baba as well. There was something going on with him that he was not ready to share with me yet. But that time was soon to come. This was not just a tour, this was a sure enough pilgrimage back into the sacred temples that were a true reflection of my covenant, once again, in another lifetime with **The Great Mother**.

I could feel the remnants of my soul getting ready to reveal, exactly what, I was not sure, but knew was yet to come. You see, in the middle of this pilgrimage, suddenly we were told that we all had to cross over this narrow strip of land that resembled a bridge, a bridge without guardrails.

Hearing this message, I came back into my body that had a major height phobia… especially when it came to crossing over narrow bridges in a car. But now we were crossing on FOOT! I had no idea where this trek was going to lead me. What if I fall off this trail and, once again, my life journey is ended before its time?! It was time to reconnect to all of me within this human form!

On the other hand, Baba didn't have this fear and was extremely curious about what was on the other side. He felt this pull to get to the other side, which he shared with me later. As I stood there watching, I witnessed all the people on this journey with us, crossed this pathway seemingly effortlessly. Wow, not me. I couldn't even take one step onto the path without this fear raging through my body. I started crying and the next thing I knew many of them were cheering, "Come on, you can do it; you can do it, Osunnike; you can do it." At that point, Baba looked back and saw that I was literally shaking and still standing on the other side.

He stretched his arms out toward me and started walking back to me and smiled nodding his head, and said, "We can do this. Just look at me." Once he got to me, he took my hands and began walking backwards along the path, while holding my hands and saying over and over again, "Babe, I've got you; just look at me."

I was also able to feel and sense that the group had all come back onto the path and was standing along the edges, whispering, "You've got this. You've got this. You've got this." When I got to the other side, we all embraced, as I apologized for my behavior the night before. They all said, "No apology necessary. This is a revelatory time for all of us." Truer words could not have been spoken. Now, on the other side, we began to explore cavernous parts of this sacred land and, as I began to go deeper down, I began to remember.

*As I surrendered to the full remembrance of this truth, in the rush of what seemed like an eternity, I felt my rage, pain, jealousy, sorrow, shame, guilt and the disappointment of so many failed reunions with my Higher Self, now being cellularly cleansed from the bowels of my mind. One by one, purifying and healing those painful memories of my tragic lifetime as **MaFaRaEL** in Lemuria, which were embedded within the cellular memory of my womb. I was finally liberated from the emotional pain of these old memories as Vonnia - a wise seeress and spiritual oracle for humanity.*

In a deeply penetrating state of trance, I began to witness, the features of her life beginning to unfold like a panoramic movie before my eyes. In a whirlwind of stillness, I could see and recognize her strong broad face with my sharp keen inner eyes, the same inner eyes that allowed her to traverse the three worlds in the blinking of our deep brown eyes.

As our souls merged, I carefully slipped into the body temple that once enclosed her spirit. I remembered how I could feel their angry breath of raw fear breathing down upon my heel's way before my capture and long before they brutally severed my tongue to silence the prophesy of the sacred oracle that

> *effortlessly passed from my lips and then gutted out my womb in hope of extracting and eradicating the power of The Sacred Feminine Mysteries that I and the other Ancient Mothers of Mu had vowed and devoted our entire lives to safe keep.*
>
> *I could hear my silent screams echoing in the wind as they violently and viciously tore from the inner sanctum of my womb my innocent baby girl whose tormented soul would be lost in the fibers of bewilderment, endlessly searching for its completion lifetime after lifetime.*

My spirit was reawakened as I listened with my heart to the ancient whispering echoes of the Ancient Mothers… Do you know who you are…

Yes, I remembered with laser precision excavating the dormant memories as a high priestess, shaman, seeress and midwife of the Sacred Feminine Mysteries Initiation that I began thousands of years ago in Lemuria and Peru.

As I shared this horrific and enlightening memory with Baba, he held me close and shared that he remembered this ordeal as well. He realized that he too was a part of that lifetime as a priest shaman and was unable to save me from this brutal attack from the conquistadors as they tortured and savaged so many sacred feminine wombs and the sacred Machu Picchu land. Jorge, our shaman guide also shared that over the years most of the mummies that were extracted from within the underground caves were female, and there were mystical stories that they may have been Priestesses and Sacred Prostitutes journeying into the higher realms with alien cosmic beings.

Reconnecting to those memories in the sacred arms of the Ancient Mothers, and the safe space that Baba held for me, allowed me to release the torment of being fragmented. This journey back home to "myself" reawakened my ancient womb memories from a place of compassion. I was now encouraged to re-embrace, re-embody, and reignite with the innate power of my sacred womb, whether it was physically there or not.

My womb was not empty. It was a unifying circular tapestry of wholeness that contained the medicine to fully weave and integrate all my lifetime experiences into one truth – the truth of Unconditional Love.

Yes, I Answered My Calling to Rebirth the Sacred Feminine Mysteries

Upon returning home, I knew that I was created, chosen, and called to now return, in this lifetime, to spiritually midwife "chosen" women – in answering that unrelenting Inner Spiritual Calling to remember, reawaken and rebirth their Sacred Feminine Mysteries covenant with **The Great Mother**, in service to humanity, through their priesthood.

Yes, within nine months of listening to the Ancient Mothers and receiving the continued words from Baba, "You are not alone. I will guard the door, while you work your magic.", through that magic, I rebirthed the Sacred Feminine Mysteries Priestess Initiation – Passage into **The Great Mother**. This was an initiation journey uniquely designed to rekindle and excavate, from the belly of their souls, the dormant memories of the power of the Sacred Feminine Mysteries entrusted to "chosen and called" women by the Ancient Mothers of Mu (Lemuria).

I came to realize that the Ancient Mothers of Mu, my spiritual guides are the keepers of the Ancient Serpent Wisdom. They are the spiritual midwives entrusted with the responsibility of assisting All of humanity in our spiritual rebirth from the cosmic womb of **The Great Mother**. They are also the spiritual guardians for humanity who represent and uphold the integrity of our Earth Mother.

Many ancient mythological legends refer to the lost sunken continent of Mu (Lemuria), as a highly spiritual motherland, which physically existed approximately 104,000 years ago and greatly influenced the dualistic nature that governs our universal cycles of time. During the civilization of Mu, the Sacred Feminine Mysteries Initiations took a lifetime to complete. However, I was called to midwife those called in this lifetime with a conscious desire to remember their divine covenant with **The Great Mother** and relationship with The Ancient Mothers of Mu, who still exist today within the spiritual realm to guide us in reactivating the Serpent Wisdom within. The Serpent Wisdom is deeply embedded inside the cellular memory nestled within the cavern of the womb and contains the circle of life blueprint, which reveals the mysteries of birth, life, death, and rebirth. This timeless cellular umbilical cord is not only the divine link between you, your birth, and ancestral mothers, but to **The Great Mother** and to the remembrance of your spiritual lineage, legacy, divine purpose and Asé, Feminine Power.

All the different paths along my spiritual journey, this lifetime, had been designed to reactivate my feminine power and innate knowledge of who I truly Am – A Sacred Feminine Mysteries midwife and unifying bridge. The Sacred Feminine Mysteries Initiation was divinely designed to reach the women who may also have heard the whispered echoes of an ancient voice calling to them. Or possibly they have had flashbacks like I had, of past life memories involving ritualistic initiations, as a high priestess accomplished in the art of sacred sexual union and alchemy. Maybe, you've experienced present lifetime out of body sensations and situations, where your natural innate knowing, from your lifetimes in the ancient temples, as a midwife, herbalist, shaman, energy healer, dream interpreter, Seeress and oracle reader continues to surface. Better yet, what about those numerous "other worldly" spiritual readings you've had that reveal your natural and perhaps, still dormant, abilities in the visual and performing arts doing sacred dance, writing, drawing, sculpting, and painting.

Finally, there may be those vaguely familiar daunting images of being a warrior priestess or just a subtle knowing that you once ruled as a queen in leadership of an empire. Maybe, there is something ancient and longing to come forth from inside the darkened womb calabash that contains your soul blueprint. I am so grateful that I listened and have been able to midwife so many women back into the passage of **The Great Mother**.

Chapter Nine
~ Yes, I Know Who I Am ~

My Osun was guiding me to look into the mirror of myself and to see I am my mother's daughter. As I prepared to go to the next level of healing with women and their wombs, I knew that it was time for me to go into the cave of my existence and remember my true womb story so that I could rewrite my life story, because NOW was the time.

Sure enough, I got a call from one of my drama therapy mentors in Boston inviting me to attend a 10-day intensive back in the city that was the backdrop for my physical birth this lifetime. Usually, when I returned to Boston, it brought up so many old and painfully unresolved memories. But instead of the usual dread and doom of this return to the city that gave 'birth' to so many of the fragmented aspects of me, I now felt myself breathing in an air of new beginnings fueled by a long awaited and greatly needed sense of closure.

Mind you, this psychodrama transpersonal therapeutic intensive that I agreed to show up for was designed to guide me through a rebirthing opportunity just several days after my birthday. I might also add, it was not too long before the auspicious summer solstice, and I would get to spend quality time with my mother. What had I gotten myself into?! Sure enough, I was getting ready to go deeper and, I intuitively sensed that this intensive would herald in a transformative experience all within ten days.

I also felt that this group of participants had been chosen specifically for me. I pondered to myself, how could Saphira have known what I personally needed? You see, it was so important for me to feel safe – and it was – like magic from the time I arrived until the last teary goodbye. I felt very strongly that all the participants had worked as goddesses in the 'angelic realms' many times before. Somewhere inside of me, I knew without a shadow of doubt that these were wise women that the universe was bringing back together to do very sacred work – transpersonal rebirthing work.

I was extremely intrigued by the subject matter that we would be dealing with during this training –pre-birth and birth trauma. Wow, how exciting, I thought. Especially, after the energetic healing connected to my Peruvian other lifetime womb trauma. This was also the work that I had been doing for a few years, now in my private practice, with my clients in Kentucky. I certainly knew a lot about that topic.

The first night of the intensive, the very first exercise we did was reconnecting with an ancestor and allowing that ancestor to introduce us to the other participants and share a secret about us. That exercise was the most powerful of all the exercises that I participated in during the intensive. It set the stage for some deep reflective work during the intensive. It reinforced the powerful spiritual connection we have with our ancestors, and for me, ancestor reverence is a major part of my spiritual tradition.

Also, during the intensive process some of my personal challenges, such as struggling with how to infuse more creativity into my spiritual healing work with my clients, the overwhelming emotions that I often felt in connection with human suffering, and most importantly, not always remembering to replenish myself and strengthen my spiritual resolve, were being highlighted. However, what was so exciting was how my ancestor, who was called in, began to remind me that the Ancestral Cellular Memory Healing work that I had been guided to do with others could be used as a healing balm for global healing and transformation. To my surprise, the ancestor who came forth that night was Maathra from my first sweat lodge ceremony and who often visited during my ancestral work. I began to think that maybe she was perhaps one of my 4th or 5th generational ancestors from my matrilineal line. She presented herself as a powerful Medicine Woman who was guiding me to weave together the fragmented remnants of my soul into a rich tapestry of absolute authentic truth. To see her within my personal mirror of self, helped me to realize that she was somehow vital to my tapestry.

"Maathra" by Dara Imani Bayer

After calling forth this ancestor, we were guided to call in next our team of archetypal totem superpowers, to support us in rebirthing the aspects of ourselves that may be stuck or undeveloped. For me, the butterfly, mermaid, rainbow serpent, and dragon flashed before my eyes effortlessly. What made this even more exciting for me was that these totem superpowers were also aligned with the elemental energies connected to the earth, air, fire, and water. The serpent connected me to the earth to better ground myself. The mermaid connected me to the water element, which represents our human emotions, as well as instincts. For me, this was a deeper opportunity for integrating the different stages of consciousness. My sisters helped me to see and feel that the mermaids' fins representing the left and right sides of my body were out of balance. The fins revealed that there was a disconnect. Perhaps, I was not trusting or honoring my instinctual body enough, not honoring my feeling state. I realized that the mermaid archetypal totem was helping me to see that there was a disconnection between my heart (passion – heart's desire –) and my body. I was needing to bridge the gap between my feminine and masculine, my spiritual essence, and my physical body – intellect and spirit.

This was also an opportunity to rewrite the ancient myths associated with the mermaid/siren depicted in Greek mythology, as a seductive destroyer of sailors. Whereas the more accurate mythology represented them as the fierce keepers and protectors destined to prevent those pirates seeking to rape and pillage the treasures embodied within the womb of the ocean by any means necessary.

This rebirthing was requiring me to continue weaving together the fragmented threads of my own inner feminine and masculine energies. The rainbow serpent was there to assist me in knowing that I was ENOUGH, whole, and complete. It was showing me that I needed to become more interconnected within the womb of me, the conscious embodiment of me – this knowing reconnected me to the earth element that is also one with the sky.

For years, I saw myself as a rainbow-colored butterfly, and born as a Gemini, I was already an air sign, free, delightful, and mystical – that was me, flying free. However, the dragon connected to the element called fire, and was a little more challenging. I think it had more to do with my unexpressed and to some extent disconnection to this ancient RAGE that I began dissolving in Peru. With the loving support of my sister community, I was determined to continue transmuting this ancient venom so that it would not destroy my rainbow-colored butterfly. This bittersweet, wild, tender, and splendidly passionate fierceness was all a medley of me. The archetypal elemental messages coming through was that perhaps my soul's tapestry is not the beautiful, ideal, sweet image, I would like to envision. Maybe, it's made up of the remnants, the pieces that have been salvaged like the pieces used in making a quilt. Each piece has its own story. Maybe, my quilt was to become a blending of the dissonance, the potential possibilities, could be's, maybes, shall be's to all be woven together with what is right NOW, so that I consciously co-create what can be NOW. This went back to my honoring the imperfectly perfect rendition of me.

Six days into the ten, I felt within my womb the pushing and pulling of an ancient new birthing about to happen NOW. It was time and, one by one, we all had the divine opportunity to be rebirthed. During my experience that night, I heard myself saying out loud…

Anxiously I waited

This time
For my turn
My turn to be birthed – re-birthed
Consciously this time
Assured to remember
My sacred connection with you – mom – with you
We gathered – the women
In sacred circle
Adorned in beautiful reams of celestial silks
Spiritually and intuitively my soul began retracing the yellow brick road
Home from the Comic Womb of God into your womb
Consciously chosen
And always remembering
my way back
These special women who were midwifing my rebirthing somehow and someway began to embody the Ancient Mothers and they whispered, – just follow the sacred sounds
Just follow
We are here to guide you in
Adorned with the hue of all races, spiritual knowing
and the universal sounds of love
Encircling my soul with a vibration
resonating deep within
my heart
as drum
harp
a chorus of celestial voices
ushered me into
my mother's womb – my earthly home

Wow!! Some very profound revelations resurfaced during this

rebirthing experience designed to continue unearthing my cellular knowing. I began to silently scream... YES, as I began to remember MY womb experience.

I needed to re-experience this birth
I needed to return to the perfection of
Myself – whole within myself
Remembering my true and essential Self
cradled in love while embracing all my emotions
as sacred – as sacred
How do we forget?
Why do we forget?
It wasn't her fault that I forgot who I AM
I know that now... my rebirth allowed me to know that
Now
To reclaim the intimacy lost over time
With you mom
In your womb
I forgot
Did she forget how I was to show up in this lifetime as her daughter?
Did you really want me, mom
Did you choose for me to come
Did you know me – want me
Am I really my mother's daughter
And what does it mean to be your daughter

And like a movie screen, there it was... the original remembrance.

What a gift
This healing reclaiming work – I mean
Allowing this adult self to reconnect with the womb that
I thought for so long

Rejected me
Didn't connect with me
Abandoned me
Forgot the true meaning of me
Now – this time – once again
We can do this again – we are going to do this again – from a place within of true knowing, mom

I am consciously rebirthing my spirit
Whole and complete into this earthly existence at this time
as mother, artist, healer
Healer – healer – here to re-consecrate, re-unite
and celebrate the wombs of those mothers
and daughters who have forgotten
Forgotten their sacred essence – their creative genius – our collective creative genius

As a feminine being of golden, violet light I carry
the flaming legacy of our ancestral mothers
Warrior women, medicine women, priestesses, and visionaries
within my womb
I consciously choose to rebirth my self
into the Knowing
that I Am – God/Goddess
Today this is my reality

I was truly there. I was really REALLY reliving and remembering the Absolute Truth of me...

Witnessed by the sacred circle of women
My mother adoring me
Affirming me
My father flowing in earnest tears

in awe of me
My brilliance
My efficacy – my purpose clearly seen
Heralded – celebrated and reflected back to me
in harmony within my community

I no longer live in fear
I live moment to moment
in the orgasmic embodiment of my own rapture
Repeated as a daily mantra of truth
Ecstatically danced
Sweated out from every pore
My bones inhale the knowing of my stellar origins
Exhaling all illusions of limitation and inauthentic realities
In my sacred calabash
I now carry in the medicine of wholeness
for those who have been lulled into a fragmented reality

We will dance in the universal spirit of oneness
Re-birthing one another in the image of God
While reclaiming honoring our unique soul blueprint

This is the dance of the womb
That my mother forgot
That I forgot
I remember…

Amazing! I was so glad to relive this revelation, remembrance and reconfirmation of my mother's sacred womb holding and acknowledging my original greatness, while she was still alive. I didn't really know what happened at my physical birth that made me disown my feminine power – that made me doubt my own creative genius. But now I knew that she intuitively knew my greatness every time she asked me, *"Do You Know Who You Are?"* She knew the greatness that I had forgotten. Yeah, it's amazing what the cellular body remembers, and the ego body lulls you into hiding, burying and finally forgetting.

In reframing my experience of my birth, I allowed myself to not only re-enact the birthing process, but to have the kind of intimate closeness and deep dialogue, I always craved for with my mother before she returned into the ancestral realm. I had so many unanswered questions that had shaped my current image of myself. The rebirthing process gave me an opportunity to dialogue with her, not just as the baby in her womb, but our spirits revealed the mysteries my wounded self-needed to know – to heal – NO – to transform not only myself but the memories of our relationship. Granted – my perception was a distorted one. We did choose each other. But again, it got distorted. Or did it? Maybe that distortion was all a part of our soul's karmic entanglement and intergenerational unresolved womb trauma.

However, I reached out, over, and back into the unseen realms, where my soul was suspended, and called back into myself the vital and necessary fragmented pieces of myself needing to re-connect with the wholeness that I originated from. And - Beginning with the End in Mind – started to rewrite my story.

I choose to reach inside and truly recapture the essential essence of me.
I choose to know beyond the shadows of doubt that plagued my heart that I am no longer embracing the illusion of me.
I choose to climb out from inside of me sanctified, purified, and glorified.
I choose to be able to walk in the light of my own luminous shadow

shaking away the primordial dust from lifetimes of forgetfulness.
I choose to rejoice in my own language
speaking in the tongues of my own ancient reflections
mirrored to me through the eyes and the grace of the Beloved.
And to finally know with unshakable knowing that I am the chosen one for my purpose at this time to be artistically manifested each and every day.
I choose to not want this longing anymore.
Now is the time for me to know that I am all that I have ever wanted.

I also came to understand my mother's work as a teacher, missionary, prophetess, hands on healer, and social worker. I saw how her work was nurtured by her unwavering commitment and covenant to God, and how it wasn't different from my work as a priestess of Osun, seeress, energy healer and my covenant to **The Great Mother**. I also began to revisit memories from a different mindset, and saw that Mom and Nana, more than likely, had their own unresolved and perhaps distorted womb traumas. Traumas or not, they served their purpose in many phenomenal ways, and shined their work in the world as a mirror for me to honor and live my original purpose from a place of resilience not just survival.

Mom you were there… in the beginning
Chosen
as the sacred vessel
for me
to incarnate within

Purified and
glorified
you saw me in all of my
splendor…
My rainbow of light
Yet, you knew
that retaining my brilliance
would be my earthly plight
So, in the beginning…
your holy womb was carefully chosen
in support

of my sacred journey
Sanctified in the blood
of our ancestral mothers
whose spirits would someday
rise again
within my womb

Like the phoenix
I rise
from the ashes
of my own darkness
to enlighten my way home
in a magical reunion
with Self
Mom… I humbly pay homage to your holy womb…

As I rose from out of those ashes, out of the darkness into the light of my Self, it was necessary to continue to witness the dark/shadow and allow myself to integrate my light and darkness in my continued quest for balance and union from the inside out.

Ultimately, it all served as a reminder for me to "live my life" fully and authentically in each moment in honor of my gifts and life's purpose in service to humanity – without apology.

Now Back in Kentucky

A few short day after returning to Kentucky, Maathra (the Ancestor who continued to loom around me) said, "*Do YOU Really Know Who YOU Are? Why Kentucky and why your perfect sacred union has been so essential here and now? Listen, now is the time!*"

Well, I was willing to listen and to know from the inside out more of who I AM this time. I was also trying my best to travel to India with my "Up from Silence" theater mentor Bobbi who was doing amazing dramatherapy healing work with women survivors of sex trafficking.

After the powerful womb work that I had experienced, I wanted to share this creative healing process with these women. I felt so called to this opportunity and frustrated for not being able to go with her because it was so soon after returning home. I offered my apologies, and she lovingly said to me "calm down Osunnike. Just work in your own backyard for now."

"My own backyard, really Bobbi, I live in Kentucky" was my retort. To my amazement two days later I saw a clip on the nightly news talking about "sex trafficking" in Kentucky.

You've got to be kidding I thought, here in my own backyard.

At that point I delved deeper into local sex trafficking, and came to find out that this was big time in Kentucky. Yes, Kentucky was one of the top five states for this heinous crime.

While trying my best to wrap my head around this new knowing, Maathra continued to appear. During these times I would experience an internal revolution that felt like what I experienced my first night in Kentucky at the Java House, which was now screaming to be evolved.

I had to get to the core of this.

So back at my ancestral altar, "Who are you?" I silently screamed. "I need to know who you are, Maathra, so that I know the answer to the question you are silently screaming, 'Do YOU Really Know Who YOU Are' and "Why Kentucky?' and why your perfect sacred union has been so essential here and now?"

"Listen, now is the time."

After what seemed like hours of sitting there, with in the luminous darkness, I was guided to go to Ravens Run, a nature sanctuary that Baba and I loved hiking along. However, when I arrived, I was guided to go on a different trail. I was shocked and amazed because the trail that Maathra and the Ancient Mothers were guiding me toward, I had never seen before. How could that be? It was right next to the parking lot and the name of this trail was called Freedom Trail. Why had I never noticed this sign before. I had so many questions that I wanted to ask someone. I needed Baba to help me understand what the hell I was getting ready to walk into and along. I took a super deep breath, did some silent chanting, and stepped onto the trail. Wow… it felt familiar, and I felt like there were spirits calling me to move onto parts of the land that were not a part of the trail. The more I listened to the familiar sounds calling to me to step off the trail, the more I felt the need to go home cleanse my body and my womb at my shrine. And I did.

Once I finished with the womb rituals, I began to feel that there was a connection between Maathra and Ravens Run. What on earth was I getting myself into? And, lo and behold, the answers begin to reveal themselves. As I begin to regress, Maathra began to reveal herself for real! For real! I saw, felt, and experienced that we were the same physical being at Ravens Run, and the same spirit, I saw in my first sweat lodge ceremony with Baba. There, she was much younger and a slave at the Prather plantation at Ravens Run. My heart and my mind were racing. All these years, here in Lexington Kentucky, Baba and I never knew that on this sacred land, there were remnants of a plantation at a place that we walked along again and again.

"This can't be real!" I screamed out, and as I caught my breath, I realized this is real… I really was Maathra. It felt like I was watching a movie of a slave plantation. But then, I realized this wasn't a movie. It was in real time and I, Maathra, was a slave on this plantation. And then, the story unfolded right before my eyes.

I was of Native American and African origins. My mother was one of the first Igbo enslaved ancestors brought on the slave ships from Nigeria. She was radiantly resilient, no matter what. She would tell me each and every day who I really was and where I originated from. My father was a Cherokee warrior who was determined to reclaim the land that his people were the ancient caretakers of and restore the freedom of the enslaved ones or die trying. I was remembering as a child my mother slipping me into the woods late in the night to see my father and hear his promise of freedom whispered into my ears. She along with my father were determined to free the people. These memories were daunting and liberating at the same time.

No, no, no. PLEASE, no. The slave master found out that my revolutionary mother, who was preparing me for our journey into freedom, was taking me into the woods in the late-night hours to see my father, as they were determining the best routes toward our freedom.

I couldn't believe what I was seeing next. This sacred vessel, who not only birthed me and nursed me from her royal breast, was determined that my true story was not of being a slave. But the slave master wanted all of us, and especially me, to have a whole different story.

As her punishment, my beautiful African mother was repeatedly raped and then set on fire and slowly burned to death in front of everyone. I don't remember if I ever got to see my father again in that lifetime. But I did remember that, as Maathra, I developed my own integrated strategies for survival and wellbeing as a medicine woman, birth doula, midwife, and **MaFaRaEL**.

Based on the horrific tragedies, rapes, hangings and the "breeding boxes" that were happening throughout Kentucky to the enslaved women, children, and men, I as Maathra in that lifetime used my physical, mental, and spiritual medicine to circumvent as many of those atrocities' as possible, no matter what.

It felt like this medicine was being downloaded and poured into me from a kettle of ancient wisdom brewing somewhere within the stars – the Star of the White Sand. I intuitively knew this was for the younger ones that were forced to breed in those boxes and this medicine also, helped some of them to release those souls naturally and caringly. That slave master would then decide that they were not fertile enough to breed this next generation of enslaved ones. This was my way of keeping their wombs sacred if I possibly could. The medicine was also a choice that many of the women could have under these dreadful circumstances. The medicine additionally strengthened their mind, bodies, and spirits to ensure, if they chose to bring this soul forth, that child would know the absolute truth of who they are and why they are for generations and generations to come. Because these plantation men saw our sacred wombs as breeding pits, and our children as breed cattle, I was committed to using my medicine to eliminate this tragedy and turn this story around, by any means necessary.

Oh, my goddess, did I lose my sacredness, when I chose to use my body, my womb, my sexual energy, to try and keep that slave master and the men, who chose to remain attached to his vicious leash, from violating our children. These men were gifted with medicine or poison given their choice. These remembrances where liberating and burdensome at the same time. I also began unraveling an even deeper complexity with Clarence, son of the slave master and an African mother, who chose to surrender her fighting nature and look for another path toward freedom. In a major twist of things, I couldn't believe that as Maathra, I somehow loved Clarence, unfortunately, in a way that I could not fully embrace. The slave master's son had grown in love with me and I with him, but I knew I could not get distracted because I was on a mission to help free our people. This was making me absolutely crazy because I knew this man from a sacred place, all too familiar, and yet unknown.

He would sing love songs to me and write poetic notes full of forever after promises. He acquiesced to the slave master, who didn't love him or treat him like his son yet put him in place as one of the overseers of his own people. He told me he was mesmerized by the sacred feminine mysteries I embodied.

I had to make a choice because I couldn't wait for him to make his best choice. My choice was saving these women and these girls from the trauma, the pain, the torment that was happening to their wombs. I developed womb medicines, sacred chants along with healing and liberating stories to help restore their vibrancy and determination on their journey toward freedom, whether he was with me or not. My choice was freedom, and I was going to use my medicine to keep those, who made the best choices, moving toward that freedom trail. This was a choice that I also would make for the soul that me and Clarence had conceived. Clarence had to choose who he really was or who he was going to settle in as.

Then I saw the slave master coming our way…

Marsh John: Clarence Boy, how ya feeling?

Clarence: Marsh John, Ahm ailing. That broken axle cut ma laig pruty bad

Marsh John: Yeah, I know. But I'm going to need you on your feet in two weeks to get that harvest in.

Marsh John: Now Maathra, you know I've let this be a safe place for your people. I can continue to make sure that ya'll can be here if Clarence can get back to work as my overseer. I'm going to need you to get him back on his feet. Now, I'm depending on you to do that. I gotta go. I'll be back tomorrow.

I could hear and feel the heavy silence.

Clarence: You gonna fix me up ain't you pretty lady?

Maathra: You gonna die.

Clarence: What you talkin' about, you heard what Marsh John said, you spose to fix me up!

Maathra: You gonna die…

Clarence: I know you can use some that dark medicine you got to heal me up.

Maathra: Yea, maybe and maybe not.

Clarence: Ahm gonna have to tell Marsh John if you don't do *what he say.*

Maathra: *Then you really gonna die now.*

Clarence: *You really gonna let me die? You know how much I love the smell of you and your long brown hair.*

Maathra: *Yea, well that ain't love Clarence.*

Clarence: *The devil in you gal.*

Maathra: *No, the devil is in you.*

Clarence: *In me?*

Maathra: *Yea*

Clarence: *Maathra I need to know can you heal me for real?*

Maathra: *Yea, you know my medicine heals.*

Clarence: *Why would you let me die?*

Maathra: *Cause you Marsh John's overseer and you do his meanness and, some of yourn. As long as you're here, like this, yo people and my people will suffer. You let babies black and red starve last winter to keep Marsh John's surplus, gave medicine to Marsh John's horse's stead of ailing people, whupped that young boy of the tribe cause he didn't pick his yield, takin manish ways wit one of our girls who has only seen fifteen winters.*

Clarence: *Ahm jus doing what Marsh John tells me. What else we gonna do?*

Maathra: *Sometimes yea. Sometimes yo meanness… You gonna die…*

Clarence: *So Miz Doctor, what can I do? You tell me… Can black folks and red folks really come togetha?*

The last thing I reexperienced during that visual remembrance was that my baby girl, whose soul I chose to release, was my mother in this lifetime and Clarence, yes, Clarence was Baba reincarnated, who did everything in this lifetime to help liberate and reunite black, red, and white men and women, especially here in Kentucky, unapologetically. That was a part of his covenant.

Yes, my mother definitely knew who I was in the core of her beingness. Even though, in this lifetime, she may not have had a clear understanding about Africa and the enslavement of those ancestors. She knew about freedom. Daddy did also, and he declared from the pulpit that Ethiopia shall rise again. They used their church, which remember was in our house, their money, time, and energy to not only help those in need, but to leave a New Life legacy for generations to come.

Again, she and my father, were radical folks on a mission to restore freedom, justice, and dignity to those abused and misused, no matter what. As I began to reflect more on my ancestors from Africa to America, I knew that I came from a powerful maternal and paternal, no nonsense, ancestral lineage going back seven generations and beyond. I began remembering deep conversations with my sister, who remembered everything, about the historical powerful ancestors we originated from.

I remembered when we discovered that Nana made a choice for the benefit of our mother, when she was one or two years old, to leave South Carolina with Papa to start a new life. We later found out that papa was not our birth grandfather. We didn't know all of the details, but what we did know is that moms birth father was not a part of her life from the beginning. Nana and Papa travelled to Massachusetts and, within a year or two, brought our mother to her new home, that then became a home for so many who were homeless. Daddy's parents were from Georgia, and sent their children, when they were teenagers, up north and to freer parts of the country, as their mother's health began to fail. The intention was that the children could have a greater opportunity for success and in turn pass that success on intergenerationally.

When I saw this picture of two of my fathers' aunties, I thought to myself WHOA, they are definitely revolutionary evolutionaries!

Now, I began to truly know why in this lifetime, me and Baba, my twin soul and King, came back to Kentucky. We were now a conscious Unifying Bridge between our African American, African, Indigenous Native American, and European ancestors "a Perfect Sacred Union" prototype to co-create and rebirth a New World as part of our covenant and legacy. We also discovered through our connection with an Igbo Chief, retired professor, and author of the book "From Freedom to Freedom" who lives here in Kentucky, that some of the first enslaved ancestors here in Kentucky were Igbos from Nigeria. This knowing was right in alignment for us because our DNA test results traced us to our Nigerian ancestors.

Now, as the co-founders of The Institute of Whole Life Healing, a non-profit organization, whose mission is to creatively assist individuals in remembering their Original Greatness, Life's Purpose, and Divinity, we are committed to that mission for generations to come. We have also been blessed to have connected, as a Unifying Bridge, with the Igbo King of Kings in Nigeria, who annually provides sacred ceremonies, as a commitment to support those from the diaspora in Cleansing Away the Stigma of Slavery. The King also formally officiated Baba, as King and honored me as the Queen within our Spiritual Queen/Kingdom located here in Kentucky.

Finally, we are committed to being and sustaining the Unifying Rainbow Bridge, from Africa to America and beyond.

Finale
~ The Divine Cosmic Womb Blueprint ~

A few years after this revolutionary remembrance of this powerful other lifetime, as Maathra, with my beloved Baba as Clarence, and all the personal sacred sexual healing, womb liberation and rebirthing that I humbly surrendered into, now led me on a final "cosmic womb" journey. I didn't know at the time that this was going to be a reactivation of my human womb within the cosmic womb. As the mothers began to whisper those silent roaring echoes, I was being guided to tap into the universal and planetary electro-magnetic energy grids also known as Ley lines that were right under my feet here in Kentucky. I was shocked, I mean potent Ley lines, and portals, and Kentucky… wow!

To my surprise I found out that Kentucky has some powerful sacred portals in the Appalachian Mountains, and the Mammoth and Horse Cave sites. Once again, when I began learning more about the powerful Ley lines here in Kentucky, I was stunned. I had to reflect on Baba telling me about the powerful Ley lines he had tapped into on the sacred Native American mound where he facilitated the Sweat Lodge Ceremonies. These Ley lines have been referred to by ancient Indigenous ancestors as "spirit lines and dragon lines" as well as other terms of use.

I was realizing more and more that the intricate blueprint of our cosmic and planetary Ley lines in many ways were a synonymous reflection of our physical and energetic arterial and vein functions within the physical womb. Our ancient ancestors live in harmony with the universal and physical Ley lines. However, in these so-called new times, these powerful magnetic energetic universal Ley lines are being desecrated, and that desecration, is being experienced within many physical wombs as well.

Well, I was more than ready to consciously explore this cosmic and physical womb journey. I mean, We Are One... Right? Yes, I was listening, and delving even deeper into my own sacred union Tantric studies and practices. Sure enough, within a few weeks I was guided to attend a Tantric Sacred Sexual weekend retreat in Belgium. Yes, you heard me correctly – Belgium. Yes, Ancient Mothers, I'm listening and packing at the same time.

From the time I arrived on Thursday, until day 3 – Sunday, I was having a very difficult time. What on Earth or the Cosmo's had they gotten me into. Initially, I felt like I wasn't learning or experiencing anything new. I was the only Black person of about 25 participants, and I couldn't speak French, which most everyone else only spoke. I felt very isolated, lonely and a bit discombobulated. Yup, I was ready to head back to Kentucky or even Boston, where I felt much more connected now. However, this was not an inexpensive road trip. So, I decided to get out of my head and wallet and thank goodness I did. Because, to my surprise, in the morning of day 3, it was shared with us that later in the afternoon we would be doing very deep womb work.

I remember sensing some anxiety with these strangers as we were guided to lay on our backs in the birthing position knees up and legs open. I felt so vulnerable, so alone. Searching within my mind, why did I have to come this far to be this isolated. My answer was soon to come. We were guided to do the serpent breath much like the transformative breathwork I did long before, deep into the throat with the mouth open breathing in and out deeply and fully. The retreat team leaders moved around the middle of the space raising the energy, opening the portal, energetically guiding us through these gates, the fifth gate, the six gate, and the seventh gate. I began to breathe and rock my pelvis slightly back and forth.

Up on the in breath, down on the out breath. Head going back on the in breath coming down on the out breath.

I was guided to continue that motion. At first, I was feeling very awkward, uncoordinated, and discombobulated with the feelings of fear and anxiety beginning to mount. Almost like when I was frightened about crossing that bridge in Peru. In my head I began calling for my Baba and begging him to come and get me. Come and get me; come and get me; come and get me. Take me home; take me home. Please, please, please, please, take me home. I don't want to be here; I don't want to be here; I don't want to be here.

I could hear some of the other folks breathing, struggling, and I knew with every fiber of my being why I was there, why I was on that mat, why I was struggling, and why I was filled with fear and terror and anxiety. And, now feeling like I was pinned to this mat, I could not run, could not leave, could not escape, breathing and moving up and down, up and down, up and down.

Knowing that you, Baba, can't save me. You cannot save me this time. There is no place safe for me, right now. I had to come all this way, completely taken out of my comfort zone, completely isolated, amongst those who don't know me, those who cannot know me, those who cannot save me from myself, from the fear of my own true Sacred Feminine power.

Only you, only you, only you, only you, **Great Mother**. Only you, the womb of my origin, I must surrender to. I have to surrender. I must surrender. I need to surrender. The impulse to surrender is so great, is so strong.

And then, I was guided to commune with my love, my beloved Baba, not to save me, but to help me liberate my spirit and ascend. I felt his spirit inside of me, loving me, guiding me home to me. *Oh, thank you. Thank you for coming, not to save me, to reunite with me, as ONE. Thank you.*

And then... then the full embrace of surrender began

happening. I felt my body being stretched and pulled like a rubber band through the eye of a needle, tightness everywhere, my body compressing like I had no bones, no vertebra, no spine, just liquid being compressed through the canal, the portal of the Cosmic Mother's womb, stretched and pulled, each contraction compressing the breath right out of my lungs. Gripped with fear of not being able to breathe, forcing me to surrender deeper, surrender my very breath this very life until I was only breathing through her to her with her.

Every contraction releasing more and more and more and more and more of the human me. Oh, more of me dying, releasing, disappearing, releasing into darkness, total luminous darkness, and expansion - glistening luminescent beings of light sprinkled throughout a web of darkness. And with my inner sight, I saw the Cosmic Mother's womb, home, home, home, home, home, home. Back into the realm of the white sand luminous particles of dust sparkling and welcoming me home – the star Sirius twinkling all through me, vibrating, pulsating, I was home. And, the higher sound frequencies echoed, and reverberated throughout my entire being you are more than Enough.

As my crown opened, there was a sensation of tugging and pulling. Within me was a sense of knowing that there was a reconfiguration going on within my head, heart, and womb. Along with a vibratory frequency retuning and transfiguring like the lotus, as the light poured in from the womb of universal darkness. As this cosmic universal consciousness laid still within my womb, simultaneously, there was an even deeper sensation of movement and motion inside my womb. It was the same sensation of tuning, transmitting a deeper resonance, a healing and clearing preparing, preparing, preparing all of me, for the union of grace with Yeshua, also known as Jesus, Heru, Sango, and Shiva, the anointed One who hovering above slowly, graciously, and energetically entered inside my womb. His staff was luminous and like an electrical current ignited all my magnetic circuits. The Ley lines were reigniting my sacred feminine blueprint. As silent fireworks began erupting inside of me from this cosmic injaculation, we ascended and from above and beyond, the words vibrated and echoed inside my womb, *"In six months you will rebirth new light from the womb of darkness."* I surrendered and remembered Who I AM. Like the Rainbow-Colored Butterfly, I was FREE.

Yes, Great Mother, I'm Listening

Six months later I was called to evolve the Sacred Feminine Mysteries Initiation – Passage into **The Great Mother** that I had been spiritually midwifing many priestesses through, into the next octave. One Million Wombs United, which utilizes sacred sound vibration and frequencies to accelerate and ignite the **MaFaRaEL** blueprint and Maathra medicine to spiritually midwife those chosen women in Rebirthing the Sacred Sexual Feminine Mysteries from within the Cosmic Womb.

As a sacred feminine, Elohim – creatress and spiritual midwife, my divine covenant is to guide you along your journey in search of your authentic Self, as you look deep into the mirror of your soul and remember your origins. Breathe and remember, in the beginning, within the silent blissful macrocosmic ocean of One-ness, there began a subtle pulsating Awareness to make manifest that which is unseen and unknown from within the Unmanifested Source. Boom!!! And then, likened to a luminous spark, the divine quintessence of the Unmanifested Source is fused with the pulsating ray of Awareness. Now, encapsulated, this essence begins rhythmically spinning, drawing in its essential cosmic consciousness (the ethereal stuff you're made of) which is then majestically impregnated within the sacred cosmic incubator that we have come to experience as the "primordial womb" of our **Great Mother**.

And from within Her dark cosmic womb – which holds the divine genetic blueprint/Ley lines for creation – ALL life is imbued with this cosmic knowing from the celestial realms, which are composed of our stellar ancestors giving birth to the elements i.e., air, fire, water, stars, meteors, the sun, the moon, and planets, as well as our own planet, mother Earth, who gives birth to and sustains our mineral realm i.e., all vegetation, our animal and insect realms, right down to the hu-man species. We are all created from the same single celled blueprint which becomes a revolutionary evolutionary roadmap for the successful journey through our cycle of birth, life, death, and rebirth.

The *Tapestry of Your Soul's* journey is the beginning of your rebirth back into the spiritual and energetic remembrance of **The Great Mother**. This remembrance of who you are facilitates a "conscious" knowing that you are "in" the manifest world (the world which "you" as She co-created) and yet, you are filled with the sacred knowing that you are not "of" the world and a deep knowing that your origins reside in the unseen un-manifested realms.

Remember, as the daughters of **The Great Mother** our dark moist womb is an intricately interconnected replica of our Earth mother's womb, and the Cosmic womb of our **Great Mother**, which gives birth to ALL. "You" are birthed in Her image. Our physical wombs are naturally and energetically infused with the nucleus (blueprint) to procreate goddesses and gods. And, by accessing that storehouse of ancient wisdom deeply embedded within the recesses of your mysterious womb, you are able to manifest Heaven on Earth. Jesus knew this, because he knew from whence, he came – the holy womb of Mary – goddess and priestess of **The Great Mother**. Yes, the Sacred Sexual Feminine Mysteries reside within "your" holy womb. And as daughters, we also carry the genetic memory of our ancestral lineage within our Sacred Wombs stretching seven generations back. This is why we honor our womb and the wombs from whence we come.

Remember your womb is an exact replica of the womb of our **Great Mother** – the original womb of God the "unmanifested" Source. And from Her alchemical caldron, this entire Universe was birthed and All of Her relations; and through Her grace, She continues to nurture our embryonic divinity within Her cosmic amniotic fluid before ushering all human life from the cave of darkness into the "rebirth" of our immortal Self. That's feminine power – that's the mystery of life within the womb of the Sacred Feminine.

So how do we access this storehouse of ancient knowing? Our physical wombs are complex incubators that are designed to nurture, nourish, and evolve our mind, body, and spirit. The umbilical cord and placenta become the lifeline to ensure that the proper ingredients are delivered for optimum mind, body, and spiritual development. To tap back into the divine knowledge, wisdom and cosmic intelligence of and within the womb, we must consciously reactivate our "umbilical communication" which is our spiritual and kinesthetic lifeline to our embryonic divinity. When we tap into our divinity through this lifeline, we are tapping into our genetic antennae that brings the past, present, and future into the NOW. Thus, it gives us unlimited access to the mystery, magic and wisdom embodied within our wombs. This requires you to first recognize the Holy Spirit (feminine power) that is quiescent within your own womb. This holy womb then needs to be honored, cleansed, and brought into balance, harmony, and the natural rhythm of the womb of our Earth mother and Universal mother. This is the call of the MaFaRaEL. This was Maathra's medicine that she utilized as a natural healer.

You are not able to honor the mystery, magic, wisdom, and sanctity of your womb without first giving that honor to all the ancestral wombs going back seven generations that are responsible first for your earthly and then cosmic existence – the womb of **The Great Mother**. This sacred telepathic matrilineal pipeline stretches back through eternity and forward into infinity, thus, enabling you to not only heal the pain and trauma, perhaps experienced within your present mother daughter relationship, but that of your ancestors, while consciously contributing to the mind, body temple and spiritual wellbeing of future generations to come from you, through you, and influenced by you. However, for this pipeline to flow unobstructed, your own womb and the wombs of your matrilineal family members again need to be energetically cleared of all physical, mental, emotional, and psychic debris.

You see having an unhealthy relationship or unresolved issues with your birth mother or primary maternal caregiver (whether she is alive or has made her transition to the ancestral realm) and/or conscious or unconscious unfinished business within your mothers' matrilineal lineage can present challenges for you in reconnecting to **The Great Mother** because this negative energy blocks the natural feminine flow of life force energy. These bio-energetic genetic blockages can also contribute to the cause of spiritual, mental, emotional, and physical dis-ease. This was the lesson that I needed to complete with my womb.

My mission over these last twenty-five years through the Sacred Feminine Mysteries initiations and sacred sexual healing, and rebirthing ceremonies have been designed to consciously assist women with their sexual healing, liberation, and igniter process. It is essential to know that within your matrilineal line, you are designed to bring your feminine essence more into alignment with your Earth mother and re-experience your divine connection to **The Great Mother**, all as part of your journey home to SELF. This energetic clearing is vital for the healthy evolution of humanity. For if the womb of our Earth mother is polluted, and She is who provides the primary nutrients for our daily existence, then how can we on this human plane produce anything healthy? If your physical womb is polluted, then how can you conceive and give birth to gods and goddesses? How can you give birth to a healthy civilization and society? How can Cosmic Intelligence and the

Essence of the Divine firmly seed Itself in a polluted vessel?

I have always believed strongly that the healthier you become the healthier the people around you become, or they move out of your sphere of influence – your life. Know that as you spiritually, mentally, emotionally, and physically cleanse and purify your own womb, you are simultaneously healing and transmuting the pain, trauma, desecration, and violations held within the womb of our earth mother, your ancestral mothers, birth mother, sisters, and daughters. Through this process you will also begin to energetically contribute to the overall healing of the imbalanced feminine and masculine energies. As well as your fathers, brothers, and sons. As you heal yourself and your family, you will naturally contribute to the healing of the human family. For one mother's womb is another mother's womb and one mother's child is another mother's child.

We End at Your Beginning

What It's Like to Work with Queen Mother Osunnike – A Testimonial

I am still sitting in the healing energy of Osunnike's grace and light.

Before too much time passes, I want to share with you the vision(s) that came and the messages that came through during my profound experience on the mat at your home. Feel free to use this testimony for your archives or website or for clients who would like to know a LITTLE of what they might experience.

On 3/23/2010 I had my very first healing session with Ifa Priestess and Olorisha Iya Osunnike. I was scheduled to have a divination with Awo Koleoso but decided to have this at a separate time so that I could sit still and absorb the intense Asé of my first session with the Queen Mother.

It's important to note that I am a 20-year veteran civil rights activist, community, and world healer, Iyalocha (presiding priestess of a Yoruba temple in Denver), High Priestess of Yemoja and Ifa who has been on the battle zone far too long.

I am also a mother, grandmother of four boys, wife, sister, auntie, friend, as well as a writer, poet and journalist who uses her words to heal herself and others and to end wars and fight battles for justice. A few months ago, Orisa sent me to the back of the formation (like they do pilots who've been at war too long) for reflection, restoration, and resurrection.

Upon arriving at the temple of the Institute of Whole Life Healing, Iya Osunnike had the insight to allow me to engage her spiritual counsel. I believe it was this exchange that tore down the walls or as she put them, "the guardrails" that allowed me to open up to *consider my own healing. Our sharing was much more than talking.*

I arrived there closed, in my own self-made prison (which I thought was a place of safety and protection from the daggers of life as an activist). As we began to dialogue my heart chakra began to open, I fought back tears many times, and then my Ori (higher consciousness) began to recognize her as one of my healers. I was reminded that I was in a safe space both by her and my Egun (ancestors). She not only heard what I was saying, she heard what I wasn't saying...

Through our dialogue, Iya was able to diagnose many of the areas and levels she was being called to treat me for. She was like a doctor doing a spiritual evaluation through words, through energy being cast off through tone, body language and expression. She is profound at the art of listening and hearing with her third eye and heart chakra. To me, this is the mark of a master Shaman.

Later we ascended to the healing room. After I gave my offerings to the Orisa, I was instructed to retire to the mat, her healing mat. This was a spiritual journey in and of itself.

The mat's spiritual alignment with the shrines in her altar room, with the specific Mandalas that surround the shrine, with windows and doors in the room--only a Shamaness selected by God and the Orisa could orchestrate physical alignment to this level. I felt every beam of light moving through the altar room. When the mat work began, I was asked to close my eyes. And having my sight cut off forced me inward, forced me to align my own Ori with the spiritual surgery and surgeon that I was now in conjunction with. When sight is cut off, as we all know, the inner journey is intensified.

There are many other things I could share about my experience, but I feel intuitively that the Shaman's rituals must not be fully exposed in writing. So, I will share only those experiences which my Orisa tell me are approved for public review.

During my time on the mat, three animals came to me--they may've been Iya's totems--or perhaps they are animals that walk with me too. Perhaps these were animals which Iya recognized as my totems and called/invoked to come forward to help her do the work. They say that a truly great healer opens you up so that you can heal yourself...

There was a bear--he worked on my left breast which has always given me trouble. Being positioned over my heart has not helped it any. Being the sensitive Yemoja priest that I am, I carry a great deal of energy in my heart which my breast tends to absorb. I have set intentions not to follow the family tradition of having breast cancer. I have made it almost 50 years with clear breast screenings. I not only reject the idea of getting breast cancer just because my mother and father's sister did, I continue NOT to set up the condition for cancer in my breast by doing self-care, setting boundaries and limits, by choosing to eat right most of the time, by drinking fresh organic juice and exercising.

The bear crouched over me as he scissored out any unhealthy cells in my breast. I could feel his breath eradicating the non-cancerous tumors I'm told I have in my left breast.

Then there was a snake who wrapped itself around my Ori. He said he was Damballah. This took place as the Apetabi (Osunnike) was chanting Odu into my heart and crown chakra (that's what it felt like). I felt the snake's scales and the coldness of his skin as he cleansed my Ori of self-doubt, fear, anger, anguish, mistrust, and negating messages (both internal and external). At first, I was scared because though I respect snakes, snakes are not my favorite species. But he told me to relax, to breathe, to trust him to do what he came to do. He slithered away when he was done. His body felt heavier than it did when he arrived.

Then I felt Apetabi (Osunnike) shapeshift. I truly felt that she was no longer in the room. I felt the presence of a large, powerful leopard. Then a cougar arrived too. Then Iya shapeshifted again and became the Oshun with the red sash, the warrior Oshun Ibukole who goes to battle with negating forces. She was fighting off entities who feed on people's hearts and souls with their negativity. I felt these entities leaving my person, then leaving the room, then leaving the house.

Then the two large cats returned and worked on my digestive system, my reproductive organs, my womb, the birth canal, and the kundalini energy that flows from the base of my spine by opening up the energy there that was blocked by me watering the seeds of hurt and resentment for far too long. At this point, it felt like the mat was levitating. My body felt weightless. Yemoja arrived.

For a while I fought being mounted by Yemoja and asked her instead to help with my healing. I wanted to be present and felt possession by the Orisa would take me away from the gift I was being given. When my Yemoja comes down it is usually to do work for others and I really wanted my own time, wanted something to be all about me.

The final phase of the healing was the closure of metaphoric stripes on my back. I could feel pure light stitching these lashes closed. I could feel a spiritual salve being placed over the wounds. I could feel thorns, daggers, the imprints of fists; hate filled names (bitch, nigger etc.) on my back that had been tattooed by seen and unseen negating forces being stripped off my back, being exorcised. Then there was a spiritual hand on my back which was light, pure light, restoring the outer layer, the inner layer, the inner most layer--my soul. I fought going into a convulsive cry...I channeled that crying/purging energy into light to heal my heart.

Finally, my ancestors came. My Aunt Janice, who was an activist and frontline community organizer, who Osunnike accurately said had unfinished business with me. Iya was on the money. The night my Aunt died, I was on my way to the hospital to see her but was so exhausted from my flight that I went on to the hotel with the intention to see her the next day. She crossed over that night.

My aunt and I finally got to say goodbye. She gave me the messages she wanted me to have about my health and how to continue take care of it.

I was also given messages from Iya about my mother who crossed over in 2008. Iya shared that mom was doing light work with kids from the other side who were healing from various issues. And this made so much sense--my mother loved children. A Yemoja in her own right, she'd had taught art to inner city kids for three decades when she was a schoolteacher in South Central Los Angeles.

After a meditative resting period, I rose from the mat and went into two yoga poses. The downward dog which segued into the mountain pose. I was free...

And during that time, I did receive a few messages for Apetabi (Osunnike). One, the book must be published. Must set a date for publication. The Orisa said she is to write something about healing ancestral karma and rebirthing one's divine purpose. This is a part of my role in her life to help her birth this baby that is her book.

Two, I saw her officializing her healing modality in a clinical sense and introducing it to academia (Chinese medicine, holistic medicine audiences)

Three, I saw her becoming a renowned lecturer and writer on something the Orisa called, AARM, African American ritual medicine (combines rituals of Africa with the cultural and ritual practices from our southern roots). She would be the one to bring this modality to an international audience.

Four, I saw her getting some sort of clinical title (only for legal reasons--the medicine is already in her blood, her DNA).

Five, I saw her and Baba Koleoso's model for Orisa worship being a model for a new era of Orisa spirituality.

What an incredible journey this was. I continue to sit still in the light of Oshun's grace and power. May Yemoja bring your blessings 100,000-fold for healing her daughter/sister Oshun.

Asé, Asé, Asé

Iyanifa Ifalade Ta'Shia Asanti

Interactive Multimedia Bonuses

Get free access to thought provoking questions, never-before seen videos, sound healings, and more:

www.OneMillionWombsUnited.org/tapestry

Tapestry of My Soul Book Handout

www.OneMillionWombsUnited.org/tapestry

Tapestry of My Soul – Rebirthing the Sacred Sexual Feminine Mysteries is a dramatic multi-media showcase chronicling Queen Mother Osunnike's spiritual journey back into wholeness. This book is designed for you to creatively traverse the labyrinth of self, excavating, honoring, and celebrating the sacred treasures lying dormant within your wombs.

These interactive bonuses are to help you ultimately cultivate a mosaic of spiritual healing, personal liberation, and human transcendence.

Queen Mother Osunnike shares these additional thought, questions, and rituals with you as a mirror that can inspire you to Rebirth Your Sacred Sexual Feminine Mysteries as you explore what it means to know yourself, cleanse and purify, and live in alignment with absolute truth.

Queen Mother Speaks at the Institute of Whole Life Healing's Annual Great Mother Honoring and Celebration

www.OneMillionWombsUnited.org/tapestry

Queen Mother Osunnike speaking many years ago to the community regarding the power of the Sacred Feminine and the Great Mother.

Priest King Baba ji Koleoso Speaks to Men at the Institute of Whole Life Healing's Annual Great Mother Honoring and Celebration

www.OneMillionWombsUnited.org/tapestry

Priest King Baba Koleoso also speaking many years ago to the community regarding the Divine Masculine and living in harmony with the Sacred Feminine.

Ancient Mother Video Clip

www.OneMillionWombsUnited.org/tapestry

This video from the Omega Theatre Transpersonal Drama Therapy Training June 2007 highlights one of my stories of overcoming overwhelm and a sense of failure by listening to the Ancient Mothers who guide me back into the deeper and higher truths of myself.

It represents women who live their life story as a societal framed statistic and the ramifications associated with those labels.

Ms. Stella Bodacious

www.OneMillionWombsUnited.org/tapestry

My Ms. Stella Bodacious performance during the Omega Theatre Recovery Through Creative Arts Therapies Training and Performance June 2008 represents women who may appear to have it all together may also be struggling from internalized trauma, disempowering beliefs and negative inner self talk held onto from childhood. This performance was a combination of scripted and improvisation to show how our internal narrative can be the driving force for our external actions. The poem that the character is reading and how its read shows how transformation can happen when you begin to rewrite and re-tell the narrative associated with your life story differently, even in the moment. My mentor, teacher, colleague, Saphira Linden, founder of Omega Theater has used the Stella Bodacious video in various trainings and performance pieces around the world as a tool for healing through the arts for women.

Sacred Mantra Meditation Sound Healing

www.OneMillionWombsUnited.org/thesacredmantra

A uniquely designed Sound Healing Vibrational practice, which blends ancient indigenous wisdom and scientifically measured knowledge (global coherence monitoring) for long-term transformative results.

A universal Womb Mantra to activate, awaken, and mobilize brainwaves into harmonic resonance by revealing the more deeply embedded challenges women have faced and how to manifest the ultimate solution from the inside out.

Work with Queen Mother Osunnike

Institute of Whole Life Healing's Annual Great Mother Honoring and Celebration

Every September in Kentucky
(Open to Everyone)

https://manypaths1truth.org/

Calling all holistic healers and truth seekers longing to find that Spiritual Kingdom that reconnects them to their Original Greatness, Life's Purpose, and Divinity: You are encouraged to join us in sacred rituals, ascension ceremonies, sound vibrational healing, mind stretching presentations, heart lifting musical performances, and more.

The Institute of Whole Life Healing is a Spiritual Kingdom representative of "many paths one truth"; and Lexington, Kentucky is its spiritual home for this multi-racial, ethnic, and culturally diverse community. Our Spiritual Kingdom's primary purpose is to stand on a foundation of African and Native American spirituality in recognition of our shared ancestry and not to isolate, segregate or confine ourselves to any one ideology.

We host our Annual **Great Mother** Honoring and Celebration each September in Lexington, Kentucky. This Holy event is an opportunity for all in our Spiritual Kingdom to come together to honor **The Great Mother**, the Cosmic Primordial Womb, that holds the divine genetic blueprint for the EVOLUTION of ALL of creation.

Spiritual Aspirant Initiation (SAI)

https://onemillionwombsunited.org/spiritual-initiations/

As women, we have the innate POWER to change our world. It's time to reclaim and reawaken your dormant Sacred Feminine POWER, which is your inherent feminine birthright deeply embedded within your womb. When we as feminine beings spiritually, mentally, emotionally, and physically cleanse and purify our own womb, we naturally contribute to the healing of the Womb of our Earth Mother and our collective human family. SAI is designed to assist you in:

- ➢ Having intimate access to ancient goddess wisdom from the inside out, and authentically re-embodying the truth of who you really are as a powerful feminine being and living your life fearlessly from the inside out.

- ➢ Having a clearer knowledge base of your sacred gifts from the inside-out, as well as becoming reconnected to the natural flow of endless creativity, ignited potential and the inner guidance of when, where, and how to navigate your life's journey.

- ➢ Laying a solid foundation for beginning the Sacred Feminine Mysteries (SFM) initiation if that is your calling.

After your Spiritual Aspirant Initiation, you can expect:

- ➢ To better understand how feminine energy manifests in your life.

- ➢ How to enter into sacred communication with your ancestors, and why that is important.

- ➢ The importance of ritual and why it is the foundation for creating a powerful connection with our Earth Mother and universal energies.

Sacred Feminine Mysteries Initiation into The Priesthood (SFM)

https://onemillionwombsunited.org/spiritual-initiations/

The Sacred Feminine Mysteries Initiation – Passage into **The Great Mother** (the feminine face of God) is for those women who are ready to answer that unrelenting Inner Spiritual Calling into the Sacred Feminine Mysteries priesthood. As a Priestess of the Sacred Feminine Mysteries, you are reawakened to the realization that you are here to make practical and spiritual use of your awakened consciousness, spiritual gifts, talents, abilities, and life's purpose in the way of service to humanity and, to re-establishing your personal covenant with **The Great Mother**.

It's up to YOU to reclaim your Sacred Feminine POWER. It's your BIRTH RIGHT. Will you be ONE of the ONE MILLION to liberate your Sacred Feminine POWER so that you can live the spectacular life that you deserve and contribute to co-creating a better WORLD?

Sacred Sexual Healing, Liberation and Wholeness Igniter Retreats

https://onemillionwombsunited.org/events/

My additional training in psycho-spiritual healing, drama therapy, energy and sound healing, and the performing arts are all creatively woven into our Sacred Feminine Mysteries initiations and Sacred Sexual Healing, Liberation and Wholeness circles and retreats for women.

This too is a calling for me to spiritually midwife "chosen, called and created" women in answering that unrelenting "inner" spiritual calling for them to remember, reawaken and rebirth their Sacred Feminine Mysteries covenant with **The Great Mother** in service to humanity through their sacred gifts and priesthood.

Within these Sacred Feminine Mysteries initiations and Sacred Sexual Healing, Liberation and Wholeness Igniter retreats, I utilize the *Beginning with the End in Mind – The Evolving Self* as an interactive writing and performance model, which will ask the question… what if this role you are playing is just that – a role?

Through this mind, body, and spirit journey, I guide women, you, to re-imagine that you are really a part of a much bigger story, a cosmic story with a much greater performance and purpose… perhaps the bigger cosmic story that you are starring in, auditioned, and rehearsed for is a part of rebirthing humanity's "new story".

During these retreats, you will experientially explore and re-experience your sacred sensual and sexual essence. Through sacred ritual, you will be guided to remember, reawaken, re-consecrate, reclaim, re-embody, reunite, and ignite your sacred sexual ancient womb (yoni) wisdom, and unveiled innocence. I dare you to join us…

Private Individual Sessions

(Open to everyone)

https://onemillionwombsunited.org

Your Psychospiritual Counseling session utilizes my spiritual intuitive awareness combined with a transpersonal and holistic mind, body and spirit view of the challenges, setbacks, and confusion that you may be experiencing along your life's journey. During these sessions, I also utilize experiential practices such as breath, movement, and sound vibration to deepen and accelerate the healing process. The intention for the session is to assist you in gaining:

- Access to your spiritual blueprint and how to navigate it, bringing you greater clarity and insight regarding the things that are most impacting your life at this time.

- A deeper energetic understanding and awareness at the cellular level of the inner workings of your mind, body, and spirit and how to manifest greater levels of healing, liberation, and wholeness.

- More confidence in your inner knowing so that you are making decisions and choices that are in alignment with your highest good.

- A holistic blueprint for reclaiming your personal power.

Energy Healing & Rebalancing Session

(Open to everyone)

https://onemillionwombsunited.org

Your private energy healing and rebalancing session begins with a spiritually intuitive reading to assess where the energy is being blocked. Once we determine some of the root causes, we then move into a deeper experiential session where we begin to:

- Identify and heal the core blockages that live within your cellular body.
- Weave together the fragmented aspects of your soul's journey.
- Reassess your core values from the inside out.
- Unleash your bound up creativity.
- Heal outdated physical, mental, emotional, and spiritual beliefs and attitudes.

These healing sessions are designed to provide you with essential sacred tools, practices, and support in:

- Re-embodying new patterns of behavior and different expectations for your life.
- Creating healthier relationships with yourself and others.
- Having a greater impact in the world because you have a greater sense of who you are.
- Increasing your vitality and inner glow.
- Raising your vibrational frequency.
- Accelerating spiritual growth and emotional development.

Sacred Healing Weekend Intensive

(Open to everyone)

https://onemillionwombsunited.org

Your private Sacred Healing Weekend Intensive is designed to hold Sacred Space that nurtures your mind, body and spirit allowing you to Stop, Breathe, Listen, and Reconnect to the Divinity within. This sacred time, just for you, will offer a "concentrated" specifically designed set of cleansing, clarifying, healing, and reflecting rituals and practices that guide you back home to Self.

During the weekend, we will delve more deeply into:

- Unfolding your life's purpose.
- How to live your life's purpose with grace and ease.
- Healing old wounds and trauma.
- Gaining greater clarity on what are your greatest gifts that you are here to share.
- What am I here to give/receive

You will leave with a template for:

- A greater level of clarity about who you are, why you're here and the gifts that you bring.
- Recognizing when you need to disconnect from the things that distract you from your core essence and gifts.
- What brings you the most joy and nurtures your mind, body, and spirit.
- How to make self-care a priority.
- How to bring more balance into your life.

Sacred Sexual Healing

https://onemillionwombsunited.org

This work is designed to assist you in journeying deep into the calabash of your yoni/womb where you will remember, reawaken, re-consecrate, reclaim, re-embody, and reunite your sacred sexual womb wisdom and unveiled innocence. Your sessions can include spiritual cleansing baths, yoni cleansing and re-consecrating ceremonies, holy touch massage, intuitive spiritual readings, energy healing, breath, sound, and movement. Our sacred rituals, ceremonies and healing practices are designed to assist you in clearing the sexual wounding and armoring that exist within your sacred yoni on a cellular level by energetically clearing and cleansing your yoni from:

- Sexual trauma/abuse/incest/rape
- Ancestral sexual trauma
- Prenatal and birth trauma
- Vaginal mutilations and dis-ease
- Surgical womb procedures: fibroid, cysts, endometriosis, etc.
- Painful menstruation and childbirths
- Unfulfilled sexual relationships
- Incomplete orgasms
- Biological imbalances and infertility
- Emotional blockages and armoring
- Painful penetration and frigidity
- Other lifetime trauma

Books by Queen Mother Osunnike

https://www.amazon.com/author/osunnike

- Tapestry of My Soul – Rebirthing the Sacred Sexual Feminine Mysteries (Paperback & Kindle)
- Bittersweet: Poetic Reflections from an Ancient Contemporary Seeress (Paperback)

Collaboration Books with Queen Mother Osunnike

- Women of Spirit Share Rituals Divine: Diverse, Personal and Evolution-Empowering Stories of Our Connection to Rituals and the Divine

  https://ritualsdivine.com/product/rituals-divine/

- Iyaami: The Dawn of Lailai

  https://www.amazon.com/Iyaami-Lailai-Divine-Light-Mothers/dp/B09YRSW9BK/

- The Heart and Soul of Psychotherapy – A Transpersonal Approach Through Theater Arts

  https://www.amazon.com/Heart-Soul-Psychotherapy-Transpersonal-Approach/dp/1466973358/

- The Seed of Pure Potential (coming June 2023)

  https://www.amazon.com/author/osunnike

- The Seed of Destiny (coming June 2023)

  https://www.amazon.com/author/osunnike

Books by Queen Mother Osunnike's husband, Priest King Baba ji Koleoso

https://www.amazon.com/s?k=Nashid+Koleoso

- Reaching Black Males Through Spirituality
- The Near-Death Experience – A Vehicle of Shamanic Initiation
- Black Lotus Rising – Discourses from a Spiritual Prostitute

More Books to Support Your Learning

- From Freedom to Freedom – Journeying Back to Heal the Wounds of the Atlantic Slave Trade by Johnston Akuma-Kalu Njoku

  https://www.amazon.com/Freedom-Journeying-Atlantic-Akuma-Kalu-2014-09-18/dp/B01K94R17G/

- Abebi: We Called for Her and She Came to Us by Nailah Jumoke (former owner of the Java House)

  https://www.amazon.com/Abebi-Called-Her-She-Came/dp/1732329710/

- Iwa-Pele: Ifa Quest by Awo Fa'Lokun Fatunmbi

  https://www.amazon.com/Iwa-Pele-Search-Source-Santeria-Lucumi/dp/1482044951/

Dedications and Acknowledgements

In eternal gratitude to my Twin Flame, husband, and Priest King Baba ji Koleoso

(February 24, 1949 - February 9, 2020)

Thank you for your 21 years of support, unconditional love and being my hero, the epitome of a man of steel and velvet, and continuously guarding the door for me, now from within the Ancestral Realm, so that I can still honor my sacred feminine mysteries covenant and endlessly work my magic. **You are forever and always The Wind Beneath My Wings.**

My Parents

With love to my Earthly Parents, Naomi and William Scott – I am eternally grateful that you remembered and honored your spiritual covenant and chose to co-create me this lifetime. I will continue to honor your legacy and share the Tapestry of our Souls.

Mama Rashidah
My dear co-sister wife
January 14, 1949 – May 31, 2015

I will never forget the first time we laid eyes on each other. To this day I continue to thank you for inviting me into the family. You were a major thread in my Tapestry. Thank you for sharing your children, Jashed, Ayesha and Yasmeen, and the grandchildren Ameerah and Khari with me. I will continue to pour libations in honor of your spirit. Love you, my sister.

Ancestral Recognition

Mucho love to my Nana, Sara Fickens Drayton, and Papa Clarence Kennon Drayton and to all my African, Cherokee, and European ancestors whose names I do not remember… I continue to pour libations to your spirits. **Asé O!**

My Sons

My first son, Mesfen, warrior Priest King, ordained to cool the strife and heal the ancient wars of injustice, so that the healing traditions of our ancient mother, Ethiopia, shall rise again. Thank you for gifting me with my granddaughters Waliyah and Kamilah.

My second son, Tarik, warrior King, destined to rule with a sharp, quick sword of truth designed to restore justice and universal laws for the upliftment of ALL of humanity. Thank you for gifting me with my granddaughter Nasia.

Thank you, my sons, for choosing my WOMB to birth you.

My Sister

My sister Doreen, I thank you for being my support, and best friend all my life. Your unconditional love, sister guidance and no-nonsense life practices have been very instrumental all throughout my life. You have been the sacred living library that contains all our childhood, teenage and adult remembrances and my sister partner in reexamining and rewriting so many of those memories. I could not have lived this life this time without you. Love you forever and ever.

Gratitude and Applause

I thank, Priestesses Lisa AyoDeji Allen and Ellen Mitchell, Poet Kevin Nance, writer and director Lois Roach and author Claudia Love Muir for lending your professional ears, consultations, workshopping, and mentorship, during my writing process, and Elder Baba Don for channeling some of the Maathra and Clarence remembrances.

I extend my gratitude to Priestess and author, Dr. Alexis Pauline Gumbs, and Olorisa and filmaker Julia Sangodare Wallace for your creative and financial support. Much gratitude to Priestess Cynthia Oya Gbemi Barnes for your incredible administrative expertise.

Thank you to Laverne Zabielski and Larry Vogt for giving me the opportunity to perform a piece of Tapestry before a live audience at Luigart Art Studio.

I give thanks to Bobbi Ausubel and Saphira Linden, my phenomenal Transpersonal dramatherapy and psychodrama mentors and teachers. Deep gratitude for Iyanifa Ifalade Ta'shia Asanti for sharing her incredible healing story in my sanctuary with all of you.

The Kentucky Foundation for Women for believing in my message and providing me with an artist grant. Ravens Run Nature Sanctuary for cleansing and restoring the sacredness of the Native American Indigenous land that was desecrated and retained so many enslaved ancestors who were subjected to heinous atrocities.

To Priestesses Dara Imani Bayer (www.imaniarts.com) for your evocative artwork gracing the pages of this book, and Deniese Woolfolk (www.deniesewoolfolk.com) for your two intricate paintings that breathe extra life into my words.

Thank you to all of the Sacred feminine Mysteries Priestesses and Orisa Priestesses and Priests who honor their covenant to **The Great Mother** and live in alignment with absolute truth.

Thank you to my amazing "Oh Darling" manifesting your intentions circle, for supporting me in manifesting my editor and publisher Steph Ritz and the book that you are reading now.

To Steph Ritz, my amazing editor and publishing guru, who lovingly and creatively guided me through the completion of *Tapestry of My Soul – Rebirthing the Sacred Sexual Feminine Mysteries*. Yes, this is my heart message, which is a story that she intuitively and artistically knows can change the world.

Queen Mother Osunnike

Your Time as a Caterpillar has Expired.

Your Wings are Ready!

www.onemillionwombsunited.org

www.ingramcontent.com/pod-product-compliance
Lightning Source LLC
Chambersburg PA
CBHW050638160426
43194CB00010B/1722